The Rome of Peter and Paul

The Rome of Peter and Paul

A Pilgrim's Handbook to New Testament Sites in the Eternal City

Brian Schmisek

⚓PICKWICK *Publications* · Eugene, Oregon

THE ROME OF PETER AND PAUL
A Pilgrim's Handbook to New Testament Sites in the Eternal City

Copyright © 2017 Brian Schmisek. All rights reserved. Except for brief quotations in critical publications or reviews, no part of this book may be reproduced in any manner without prior written permission from the publisher. Write: Permissions, Wipf and Stock Publishers, 199 W. 8th Ave., Suite 3, Eugene, OR 97401.

Pickwick Publications
An Imprint of Wipf and Stock Publishers
199 W. 8th Ave., Suite 3
Eugene, OR 97401

www.wipfandstock.com

PAPERBACK ISBN: 978-1-5326-1308-1
HARDCOVER ISBN: 978-1-5326-1310-4
EBOOK ISBN: 978-1-5326-1309-8

Cataloguing-in-Publication data:

Names: Schmisek, Brian.

Title: The Rome of Peter and Paul : a pilgrim's handbook to new testament sites in the eternal city / Brian Schmisek.

Description: Eugene, OR : Pickwick Publications, 2017 | Includes bibliographical references.

Identifiers: ISBN 978-1-5326-1308-1 (paperback) | ISBN 978-1-5326-1310-4 (hardcover) | ISBN 978-1-5326-1309-8 (ebook)

Subjects: LCSH: Christian pilgrims and pilgrimages—Italy—Rome. | Christian shrines—Italy—Rome.

Classification: BX2320.5.I8 S36 2017 (print) | BX2320.5.I8 S36 (ebook)

Manufactured in the U.S.A.   10/03/17

Scripture texts in this work are taken from the *New American Bible, revised edition* © 2010, 1991, 1986, 1970 Confraternity of Christian Doctrine, Washington, D.C. and are used by permission of the copyright owner. All Rights Reserved. No part of the New American Bible may be reproduced in any form without permission in writing from the copyright owner.

Passages from Classical Authors, including Josephus and Eusebius, are taken from the Loeb Classical Library, the most recent translation of each, unless otherwise indicated.

Passages from the Latin Vulgate are taken from: Fischer, Bonifatius, and Robert Weber. *Biblia Sacra: Iuxta Vulgatam Versionem.* Ed. Quartam Emendatam.. ed. Stuttgart: Deutsche Bibelgesellschaft, 1994. Image of map on page 22 used with permission from Oxford University Press.

Contents

Acknowledgments | vii
Preface | ix
Abbreviations | xi

Part I

1 Peter and Paul in Rome | 3
2 Brief History of First-Century Rome | 25

Part II

3 The Vatican Area | 47
4 Colosseum, Saint Clement and Environs | 66
5 Pauline Sites Outside the Walls; Appia Antica | 110
6 Synagogue and Environs | 133

Appendices | 147
Bibliography | 177

Acknowledgments

MANY STUDENTS AND COLLEAGUES have contributed to this text in numerous ways over more than ten years during which I have had the joy and fortunate privilege of being in Rome supporting summer programs with the University of Dallas and Loyola University Chicago. A colleague for ten years at the University of Dallas, whose invaluable assistance in launching our graduate ministry summer courses there was critical, and whose patience and graciousness was a model of Christian charity, is Dr. John Norris. Many evenings were spent on the piazza at the Due Santi campus regaling one another with travel tales and Roman stories over wine and sometimes grappa. Those times made this book better. Fr. Patrick Madden, another CUA Biblical Studies PhD, whose Doktorvater (the late Rev. Joseph Fitzmyer, SJ) was my own, is an insightful and joyful traveling companion and colleague, regularly offering translations of monuments and inscriptions. My own translations of some Latin included in the appendix of this book benefited greatly from his keen eye. His language ability far surpasses my own and he was gracious in his helpful suggestions for my translation of the Passion of the Saints Processus and Martinianus in the appendix. Moreover, he generously agreed to have his own notes for translating inscriptions and monuments included here as an appendix. Additional useful comments and helpful suggestions came from an Italian colleague at Loyola University Chicago, Dr. Edmondo Lupieri. For example, his careful read and pertinent questions improved my translation of Pope Damasus' poem while also saving me from some embarrassing mistakes in Italian. Of course, any errors at this point in these texts or translations would be from my own oversight.

Among the many students and different classes, most especially the Summer 2016 class on the Rome of Peter and Paul with Loyola University

ACKNOWLEDGMENTS

Chicago Institute of Pastoral Studies (IPS), Paula Kowalkowski and Tim Lankford caught early typos. Other students at IPS also assisted in various ways. Gosia Czelusniak developed the diagram for the stuccoes at St. Peter's that depict his life (see 55 below). Sarah Layli Sahrapour helped with some research especially regarding the "inter duas metas" legend and tracking down some ancient sources. Marlen Sotelo transcribed the Latin version of the Passion of the Saints Processus and Martinianus, Martyrs. And of course the entire editorial and production team at Wipf & Stock were professional and attentive throughout the whole process.

This short book is the product of many voices, questions, responses, and insights over the years. My gratitude and appreciation goes to all students and colleagues whose shared time in Rome contributed greatly to this endeavor.

Preface

THERE ARE LITERALLY THOUSANDS of books that have been written about Rome. Classicists, archaeologists, historians, biographers, art historians, engineers, architects, and more all have an interest in Rome. The city is a starting point or at least a touch point for so many fields of study. There is much more in Rome than we will ever fully address. Some visit to see its aqueducts, others visit the churches, still others want to see masterpieces of artwork, or study the city layout and how it grew. Some like to see evidence of the Risorgimento while others are interested in the place where Il Duce gave his famous speeches calling for war. Do we need another book on Rome? And if so, how to define its contents?

This book began as a series of notes for summer classes on the New Testament offered in and around Rome. It seemed I was a most fortunate teacher, able to combine my love of the Classics with my doctoral work in Biblical Studies, all in the Eternal City. In fact, the University of Dallas campus was (and still is) located off the Via Appia near the village of Due Santi ("two saints") a legendary site where Peter met Paul on the latter's journey into the city. And Loyola University Chicago's Rome campus is in the city proper. Each program and campus had certain benefits for students and faculty alike. Most of the students in these summer courses were seeking ministerial degrees, so the notes were developed each year with their questions and insights in mind. Much of what is in these pages reflects student questions or comments at the site. This handbook attempts to address those issues or matters that have been raised by countless numbers of ministerial students. The book is not a comprehensive guide to Rome, or even to each of the sites. Instead, as the title suggests, it is a handbook, a short guide for one who is interested in Roman sites that have something to do with the New Testament, and in particular those sites having to do with Peter and Paul.

We do not delve into each and every claimed New Testament artifact in the city of Rome. For example, this book does not address the purported heads of Peter and Paul at Saint John Lateran; we do not visit the Basilica of the Holy Cross in Jerusalem with its many alleged relics from the passion of Jesus; nor do we visit the crib of Jesus at Saint Mary Major or the Holy Stairs at "Scala Santa." Simply by listing some of the sites that we do not visit gives the reader a sense of how many possible sites there are to see. Instead, I have tried to limit the sites included in this book to the more significant churches and locales that have at least a tenuous connection to the New Testament or Petrine and Pauline legends in Rome, e.g., church of Saint Prisca rather than Saint Mary Major, or Tre Fontane rather than the Holy Stairs. Though Saint Prisca and Tre Fontane each have their own set of challenges, I deem the sites more relevant to ministerial students than either Saint Mary Major or the Holy Stairs. And yet, we include the Arch of Constantine, which admittedly does not connect to the New Testament, but it is situated between the Colosseum and the Arch of Titus. We could hardly skip it! So some may quibble with what is or is not included here.

There are two primary parts to this book, the first is a brief survey of what we know (or rather do not know) regarding Peter and Paul's time in Rome. The various sources of Pauline and Petrine legends are included in this survey as those legends will be important for making sense of many of the sites and their iconography. The second part of the book is more akin to a tour book laid out in four subsections, generally corresponding to geographical areas of the city.

The book presumes accepted majority positions among scripture scholars when dealing with background issues such as authorship, dating, provenance, the synoptic problem, the Johannine epilogue, etc. A good commentary on the New Testament, or simply the introductory material and notes in the NAB will address those issues. I will refer to the fruits of scholarship rather than rehash or re-present these arguments. In some cases, I will mention a minority opinion, but always as such. It is my hope that this brief handbook will assist those visitors to Rome who seek a greater understanding of certain sites as well as some historical background.

Abbreviations

ACW	Ancient Christian Writers
ANF	Ante-Nicene Fathers
AS	Acta Sanctorum. Antwerp, 1643–1940. Online: http://acta.chadwyck.com.
AYBC	Anchor Yale Bible Commentary
CAHS	Clarendon Ancient History Series
CIL	Corpus Inscriptionum Latinarum
CL	Catalogus Liberianus
CSS	Cistercian Studies Series
EH	Eusebius, Ecclesiastical History
LC	Eusebius, Life of Constantine
LCL	Loeb Classical Library
LP	Liber Pontificalis
MST	Mediaeval Sources in Translation
NAB	New American Bible
NABRE	New American Bible Revised Edition
NTA	New Testament Apocrypha. Edited by W. Schneemelcher. 2 vols. Louisville: Westminster/John Knox, 1992.
OCD	The Oxford Classical Dictionary. Edited by S. Hornblower and A. Spawforth. 3rd ed. Oxford: Oxford University Press, 1996.
PCPS	Proceedings of the Cambridge Philological Society

ABBREVIATIONS

PG	Patrologiae Cursus Completus: Series graeca. Edited by J.-P. Migne. 162 vols. Paris, 1857–1886.
PL	Patrologiae Cursus Completus: Series Latina. Edited by J.-P. Migne. 217 vols. Paris, 1844–1864.
TTHLS	Translated Texts for Historians Latin Series
WGRW	Writings from the Greco-Roman World
WGRWSS	Writings from the Greco-Roman World Supplement Series

Standard abbreviations are used for books of the Bible and Classical authors.

Part I

1

Peter and Paul in Rome

New Testament

PERHAPS SURPRISINGLY, THOUGH PETER and Paul are often referred to as the founders of the church in Rome, there is no direct evidence for either of them even being in the Eternal City prior to Paul's writing his Letter to the Romans in the winter of 57–58. In that letter he speaks of his desire to visit "for many years" (15:23; cf. 1:13). Part of the reason he had not visited was because of his custom not to preach where others have already laid a foundation (15:20). "This is why I have so often been hindered from coming to you" (Rom 15:22). And despite naming over two dozen members of the community (Rom 16:3–15) he never mentions Peter in this letter to Roman Christians. So it seems quite certain that the Christian community in Rome was founded by others. But by whom?

When Peter preached at Pentecost shortly after the death and resurrection of Jesus, Luke tells us there were, among many others, sojourners from Rome (Acts 2:10). If some of these sojourners were among those who were baptized at Pentecost, the Christian seed would have been planted in Rome upon their return. These Jewish Christians might have included Andronicus and Junia, Paul's fellow countrymen, "my relatives and my fellow prisoners; they are prominent among the apostles and they were in Christ before me" (Rom 16:7). To say Andronicus and Junia were present at Pentecost, and thus founded the Roman Christian community is based on circumstantial evidence at best; it would not be conclusive proof. But the hypothesis might represent the best attempt to name the founders. As difficult as it may be for us to admit, "the beginnings of the Roman Christian community remain shrouded in mystery."[1]

Written years after Paul's Letter to the Romans are the Petrine letters. Most scholars today consider 1 and 2 Peter to be pseudonymous; that is, they were written by someone other than Peter. Though 2 Peter gives no indication as to where it was written, 1 Peter lays claim to having been written through Silvanus (5:12) from "Babylon" (5:13), which is often a code-name of sorts for Rome (cf. Rev 14:8; 16:9; 18:2, 10, 21). Mark is also there. These verses (1 Pet 5:12–13) are the earliest written reference to an association of Silvanus, Mark and Peter in "Rome." Such an association, though not at Rome, is also referenced in Acts. There a certain Mary, "the mother of John who is called Mark" had a house in Jerusalem (Acts 12:12) where Peter fled upon his escape from prison. (As an aside, the chains that bound him in that imprisonment are said to be at San Pietro in Vincoli [Saint Peter in Chains] in Rome). So even though 1 and 2 Peter are pseudonymous, 1 Peter at least makes mention of the association of Peter, Mark, and Silvanus in Rome.

Mark was also known as the cousin of Barnabas (Col 4:10) and accompanied Barnabas and Paul on part of a missionary journey (Acts 12:25—13:13). However, it seems that when the going got tough, Mark got going, as he deserted them in Pamphylia (Acts 13:13). They met up again at the so-called Council of Jerusalem (Acts 15) where both Peter and Silvanus (Silas) were present. Afterwards, Paul refused to travel with Mark due to his earlier desertion (Acts 15:38). Paul and Silas went one way whereas Barnabas and Mark, being cousins after all, went another. The undisputed letter of Paul to Philemon written when Paul was "an old man" (*presbytēs*)[2] (Phlm 9) mentions a Mark (Phlm 24) as does the disputed 2 Tim (4:11). So it seems Paul and Mark were eventually reconciled. Mark's final years would have been in Rome, perhaps associated with Peter once again. Thus, the threesome (Peter, Mark, Silvanus) in 1 Peter has plausible roots in Acts.[3]

The New Testament also seems to be aware that Peter faced a martyr's death, or at least he did not die of old age. In the epilogue to the Gospel of John, what is commonly referred to as chapter 21, Jesus makes a prediction about Peter. Immediately following the "rehabilitation of Peter" where Jesus

---

1. Fitzmyer, *Romans*, 32.30.

2. The term *presbytēs* meant someone between the ages of 50 and 56. Cf. Philo, *De opificio mundi* 36 §105.

3. Cf. Elliott, *1 Peter*, 887–89.

asks three times "Do you love me," and Peter responds affirmatively three times. Jesus continues by saying:

> "Amen, Amen I say to you, when you were younger, you used to dress yourself and go where you wanted; but when you grow old, you will stretch out your hands, and someone else will dress you and lead you where you do not want to go." He said this signifying by what kind of death he would glorify God. And when he had said this, he said to him, "Follow me" (John 21:18–19).

This is perhaps the clearest indication in the New Testament that Peter suffered a martyr's death, and even so, it gives us no indication as to place. However, it does say, "when you grow old (*gērasēs*),"[4] which indicates his age at the time of his death.

In the case of Paul, we have Luke's Acts of the Apostles, the second half of which is essentially an "Acts of Paul," as he is the primary character. Acts of the Apostles concludes with Paul under house arrest in Rome (Acts 28:16). But to our modern ears the ending seems rather abrupt and perhaps not that fulfilling: "He remained for two full years in his lodgings [in Rome]. He received all who came to him, and with complete assurance and without hindrance he proclaimed the kingdom of God and taught about the Lord Jesus Christ" (Acts 28:30–31).

In fact, the ending is so startling and unexpected that at least one scholar likened it to the ending of the HBO series "Sopranos"![5] We are left wondering what happened to Paul. Was he ever released from house arrest? Was his case heard before Caesar (i.e., Nero), to whom Paul had appealed (Acts 25:11–12)? Did he eventually go to Spain as he at one time intended? (Rom 15:24)? Or was he sentenced to death by Nero? Acts leaves us grasping for answers. Other New Testament documents are little help. The last of the undisputed letters Paul writes is likely Philemon, written from imprisonment (Phlm 1, 9–10, 13, 22–23) when he was "an old man" (Phlm 9) as we noted above. Various locales have been proposed for this letter including Rome, Caesarea, and Ephesus. Scholarly opinion is generally split between Rome and Ephesus, with the latter seeing slightly more support. In any case, Paul names Timothy as a co-sender (Phlm 1) and also extends greetings from Epaphras (a fellow prisoner), Mark, Aristarchus, Demas, and Luke, "coworkers" all (Phlm 24). One has the picture of a band

---

4. The term *gēras* meant someone 57 years or older. Cf. Philo, *De opificio mundi* 36 §105.

5. Kiel, "Did Paul Get Whacked?"

of associates providing mutual support in a trying time. The embryonic movement saw one of its leaders imprisoned but his pen unfettered.

In addition to this final undisputed letter of Paul we have the "last will and testament" which is also known as 2 Timothy, and which is a letter written from imprisonment (1:16; 2:9; 4:16). Though many scholars consider 2 Timothy to be pseudonymous, there has been renewed interest in seeing the letter as authentically Pauline.[6] In such a case, 2 Timothy would have been written from Rome, after his first defense (2 Tim 4:16), where he knows his end is near (2 Tim 4:6–8). Some of those named in the letter are identified with the next generation of Christians by church Fathers, and will be of interest in our study of Rome. E.g., Linus (2 Tim 4:21) was identified by Irenaeus as the bishop of Rome who succeeded Peter (AH 3.3.3). Pudens (2 Tim 4:21) becomes the source of later legend and his purported daughters become the namesake of two churches in Rome (Pudenziana and Prassede). Prisca and Aquila are also named (2 Tim 4:19) and they too have a house church in Rome. More will be said about them when we visit that church.

Thus exhausts our review of the scanty New Testament evidence, which is silent about Peter and Paul founding the church in Rome, or even being martyred there. For those traditions we look beyond the New Testament.

Apostolic Fathers

The Apostolic Fathers are a collection of writings from Christian authors traditionally understood to have been associated with the apostles either directly or indirectly. Some of the Apostolic Fathers consider Peter and Paul founders of the church in Rome not because they were the first to evangelize there but because both suffered martyrdom there. For example, the First Letter of Clement, written from Rome in about 96 CE mentions the deaths of Peter and Paul there, in referring to,

> let us come to those who became athletic contenders in quite recent times. We should consider the noble examples of our own generation. Because of jealousy and envy the greatest and most upright pillars were persecuted, and they struggled in the contest even to death. We should set before our eyes the good apostles. There is Peter, who because of unjust jealousy bore up under

6. E.g., Johnson, *The First and Second Letters to Timothy*.

hardships not just once or twice, but many times; and having thus borne his witness he went to the place of glory that he deserved. Because of jealousy and strife Paul pointed the way to the prize for endurance. Seven times he bore chains; he was sent into exile and stoned; he served as a herald in both the East and the West; and he received the noble reputation for his faith. He taught righteousness to the whole world, and came to the limits of the West, bearing his witness before the rulers. And so he was set free from this world and transported up to the holy place, having become the greatest example of endurance (1 Clem 5).[7]

Interestingly, and perhaps a bit problematic, Clement refers to Paul "having reached the farthest bounds of the West." Does this mean Spain? It hardly seems like Rome. Still he mentions other aspects of Paul's life for which we have no other evidence: stoning, exile. We therefore read Clement with caution.

Not only Clement, but also Ignatius of Antioch, in about 110 CE, refers to Peter and Paul in his Letter to the Romans. "I am not enjoining you as Peter and Paul did. They were apostles, I am condemned; they were free, until now I have been a slave."[8] So the period of the Apostolic Fathers points to the presence of Peter and Paul in Rome, but not necessarily their respective martyrdoms there.

Apologists

While the Apostolic Fathers wrote primarily to those within the believing community, the Apologists in the latter half of the second century wrote mostly to those outside the church. The Apologists defended Christianity against persecutions and pagan accusations. Apologetic literature flourished in the second and third centuries and continued even after the political victory of Christianity in the Empire.

Interestingly, a prominent Apologist, Justin Martyr (ca. 100–165 CE), lived in Rome but never once mentions Peter or Paul having lived there, having founded the church there, or having been martyred there. Instead, Justin tells us about a Simon Magus (Simon the Magician) who is the Simon of Acts 8:9–24 (1 Apol 26). Simon Magus for centuries was known as the 'father of all heresies.' Justin's stories about Simon Magus coming

---

7. Clement, "First Letter of Clement," 5.
8. Ignatius of Antioch, *Letter to the Romans*, 4.

to Rome during the reign of the Emperor Claudius (41–54 CE) become source material for many later legends that will inform our understanding of Rome. For example, Justin says that the Romans honored Simon Magus with a statue erected between two bridges on the Tiber River which bore the Latin inscription: *Simoni Deo Sancto* ("to Simon the holy god") (1 Apol 26). This is quite a charge, and it would mean that Simon Magus made a tremendous impression upon the Romans.

But upon closer examination, it appears Justin misunderstood something, for in the Renaissance was unearthed a statue to Semo Sancus Dius Fidius, a Roman deity of oaths and treaties, worshipped on the Quirinal Hill and on the Tiber Island. The name of the deity was often simply "Sancus," but also "Semo Sancus." The appellation "Dius Fidius" is interpreted to mean, "son of Jupiter." At times the name Sancus was also spelled Sanctus. In this way, a dedication that read, *Semoni deo Sancto* ("to Semo Deus Sanctus"), was misunderstood by Christians to refer to Simon Magus, when in reality the Romans were referring to Semo Sancus, son of Jupiter.[9] But for our purposes, apart from anything about Simon Magus, Justin's lack of any mention of Peter or Paul in Rome seems to be a deafening silence.

Another early apologist was a pupil of Polycarp, Irenaeus of Lyons (ca. 120–202 CE), who writes of Peter and Paul, the "two most glorious apostles" founding and building up the church at Rome.[10] This is the first clear and explicit claim for their "founding the church," but this goes beyond the New Testament evidence, as we have seen. Perhaps Irenaeus means 'founding' in the sense of 'being martyred there,' but he does not mention their death or martyrdom. So scholars take Irenaeus' words here with caution.

Tertullian (ca. 160–240 CE) seems to be the first to place the martyrdom of both Peter and Paul in Rome:

> you have Rome, from which there comes even into our own hands the very authority (of apostles themselves). How happy is its church, on which apostles poured forth all their doctrine along with their blood! Where Peter endures a passion like his Lord's! Where Paul wins his crown in a death like John's where the Apostle John was first plunged, unhurt, into boiling oil, and thence remitted to his island-exile![11]

---

9. *OCD*, s.v. Semo Sancus Dius Fidius, which also cites Tertullian, *Apology* 13.9 as misinterpreting the Latin inscription.

10. Irenaeus, *Against Heresies*, 3.3.2–3.

11. Tertullian, *Prescription of the Heretics*, 36.

Still, the value of Tertullian's testimony might be questioned as he compares Paul's martyrdom to that of John's which involved being plunged into boiling oil unharmed. In another document from Tertullian (*Scorpiace*, 648) he alludes to the Johannine passage (21:18) about Peter's eventual death in saying that another fastened Peter with a belt when he was bound to the cross. In the same document Tertullian also states clearly that Paul was martyred in Rome.

We can eavesdrop on still another fascinating discussion from Tertullian when we read his side of a dispute with in all likelihood Callistus, who was Bishop of Rome from 217–222. Callistus issued an edict allowing those who were unchaste to receive penance and forgiveness. This was a new development in the church as heretofore that sin (adultery) was considered unforgiveable. Callistus appealed to Jesus' giving Peter the power to bind and loose. Moreover, he believed that power was passed to him (Callistus) as the church was "near Peter." For his part, Tertullian saw this as a wholly unorthodox reading and application of that power, which was given by Jesus to Peter alone.[12] For our purposes, the value of this discussion is the claim Callistus is making based on the proximity to Peter, and that is presumably his final resting place. The bishop of that church has the power that had been given by Jesus to Peter. This is clear evidence from the early third century that Peter's tomb was in Rome.

So by the time we come to the end of the third century we have seen the presence of Peter in Paul in Rome grow from not having been there at its founding (according to the New Testament) to being named the pillars of the church (Clement) who enjoined the Roman Christian community (Ignatius), who founded the church (Irenaeus) with their blood (Tertullian). But let us not neglect to mention Justin Martyr, the Apologist who lived in Rome, who strangely never mentions Peter or Paul, but does write of Simon Magus. So we are aware of the problematic aspects of the claims surrounding Peter and Paul's presence and martyrdom in Rome.

---

12. For more on this see Tertullian, "you therefore presume that the power of binding and loosing has derived to you, that is, to every Church akin to Peter, what sort of man are you, subverting and wholly changing the manifest intention of the Lord, conferring (as that intention did) this (gift) personally upon Peter?" (*On Modesty*, 21).

THE ROME OF PETER AND PAUL—PART I

Eusebius

Still other literature attests to Peter and Paul being in Rome. In the early fourth century, after the Emperor Constantine issued the Edict of Milan, granting Christianity legal status in the Empire, he requested that Eusebius of Caesarea (ca. 260–340 CE) write an *Ecclesiastical History* (abbreviated as *EH*). Eusebius also wrote a *Life of Constantine* (abbreviated as *LC*) which records various legends including the story of the apparition of the cross, by which Constantine defeated Maxentius at the Milvian Bridge. But the *Ecclesiastical History* gives an account of the church's growth from Jesus himself to the then contemporary age of Constantine. Eusebius, a friend of Constantine who also attended the Council of Nicea, preserves a number of stories from these first three hundred years, though not all are of the same quality when it comes to historical reliability. For example, he preserves a Syriac letter from Jesus himself that virtually all scholars today regard as a forgery.

Still Eusebius does preserve some otherwise lost material. For example, though we have some works from Origen (ca. 185–254 CE), many were destroyed as he was eventually declared a heretic. Eusebius cites Origen's third volume of his Commentary on Genesis in saying:

> Peter seems to have preached to the Jews of the Dispersion in Pontus and Galatia and Bithynia, Cappadocia, and Asia, and at the end he came to Rome and was crucified head downwards, for so he had demanded to suffer. What need be said of Paul, who fulfilled the gospel of Christ from Jerusalem to Illyria and afterward was martyred in Rome under Nero? This is stated exactly by Origen in the third volume of his commentary on Genesis. After the martyrdom of Paul and Peter, Linus was the first appointed to the bishopric of the church of Rome. Paul mentions him when writing from Rome to Timothy in the salutation at the end of the Epistle.[13]

The "new" information here would be Peter's inverted crucifixion at his own request. This snippet will become primary source material for artists through the centuries. At another point in his work, Eusebius gives additional information about their martyrdom under the emperor Nero and subsequent "trophies."

> It is related that in his [Nero's] time Paul was beheaded in Rome itself, and that Peter likewise was crucified, and the title of "Peter

13. Eusebius, *The Ecclesiastical History* 3.1.2.

and Paul," which is still given to the cemeteries there, confirms the story, no less than does a writer of the Church named Caius, who lived when Zephyrinus was Bishop of Rome [199–217]. Caius in a written discussion with Proclus, the leader of the Montanists, speaks as follows of the places where the sacred relics of the Apostles in question are deposited: "But I can point out the trophies of the Apostles, for if you will go to the Vatican or to the Ostian Way you will find the trophies of those who founded this Church." And that they both were martyred at the same time Dionysius, bishop of Corinth [ca. 166–175],[14] affirms in this passage of his correspondence with the Romans: "By so great an admonition you bound together the foundations of the Romans and Corinthians by Peter and Paul, for both of them taught together in our Corinth and were our founders, and together also taught in Italy in the same place and were martyred at the same time." And this may serve to confirm still further the facts narrated.[15]

So the fourth-century Eusebius is citing the third-century Caius (or Gaius) and the second-century Dionysius. The "trophies" mentioned by Caius are the equivalent of tombstones, or burial markers. The Vatican would have the trophy of Peter, whereas the trophy of Paul would be on the Ostian way, the road that led from Rome to the port city of Ostia a few miles downstream. This is significant in that the trophies (or rather tombs) of the apostles were known and likely revered as the final resting places of the founders of the church at Rome. This trophy of Gaius can be seen during the scavi tour at St. Peter's.

Earlier in this same work, Eusebius builds on the stories that came down from Justin Martyr about Simon. Only for Eusebius, Simon was met by Peter, "a noble commander of God, clad in divine armor, [who] carried the costly merchandise of the light of the understanding from the East to those who dwelt in the West" (*EH* 2.14.6). Simon was utterly defeated by Peter, whose preaching was in such demand that Mark, a follower of Peter, created the written gospel that bears his name (*EH* 2.15.1). Later, in book three of Eusebius' work, he returns to the topic of the gospels, this time quoting from Papias, who in turn is quoting "the presbyter" John, a disciple of the Lord:

---

14. The only dates we have for Dionysius, bishop of Corinth, are based on a letter he wrote to Soter, who was bishop of Rome from 166–175.

15. Eusebius, *The Ecclesiastical History* 2.25.5–8.

"And the Presbyter used to say this, 'Mark became Peter's interpreter and wrote accurately all that he remembered, not, indeed, in order, of the things said or done by the Lord. For he had not heard the Lord, nor had he followed him, but later on, as I said, followed Peter, who used to give teaching as necessity demanded but not making, as it were, an arrangement of the Lord's oracles, so that Mark did nothing wrong in thus writing down single points as he remembered them. For to one thing he gave attention, to leave out nothing of what he had heard and to make no false statements in them.'" This is related by Papias about Mark.[16]

Thus Eusebius tells us a great deal, preserving traditions and legends that would otherwise have been lost to history. Even so, we read his work with caution recognizing that not all he writes or preserves is of the same historical quality.

Apocrypha

Up to this point we have been discussing relatively standard reference works for the first three centuries of the Christian Era. But now we turn our attention to some fantastical, imaginative literature, also known as New Testament apocrypha. Though the word apocrypha literally means "hidden," these ancient works were anything but hidden. They were distributed widely and modified many times and in various ways. These works include the Acts of Peter, Acts of Paul, the Acts of Peter and Paul, the Gospel of Peter, the Correspondence between Seneca (first-century philosopher and tutor of Nero) and Paul, the Acts of Paul and Thecla, and countless other texts that were not considered "canonical" or scripture by early Christians. These works do not contain much of anything that is historically reliable. Instead, these works can be thought of "fan fiction" written by believing Christians who wanted to tell stories about their heroes. Our purpose here is not to review each and every apocryphal work, but to note those that will inform our understanding of certain legends and sites around Rome that have to do with Peter and Paul.[17]

---

16. Ibid., 3.39.15.

17. Those interested in apocryphal literature are encouraged to consult *NTA*; Eastman, *Ancient Martyrdom Accounts*; and Tajra, *Martyrdom of St. Paul*.

Acts of Peter

The Acts of Peter, dated from 180–190,[18] was composed in Greek and consists of the following:

- Paul's departure from Rome to Spain (chs. 1–3)
- Simon Magus' arrival in Rome (chs. 4–6)
- Bouts between Simon Magus and Peter (chs. 7–29)
- Martyrdom of Peter (chs 30–41)

A brief summary of the narrative is as follows: Simon Magus comes to Rome and converts many Christians away from the truth. "[A]ll fell away except the presbyter Narcissus and two women in the lodging-house of the Bithynians and four who could no longer go out of their house."[19] Peter comes from Jerusalem by ship, converting the captain along the way. Once in Rome, the crowd clamors for a battle between Peter and Simon. Peter gives a dog the gift of voice to speak for him, calling Simon out of his patron's house, where he has been staying. Upon seeing the talking dog, Simon's benefactor converts back to Christianity and begs Peter's forgiveness claiming that Simon had persuaded him to erect a statue with the inscription, "To Simon the young God." This story of course is a probable echo of Justin Martyr's claim cited above that the Romans had built such a monument.

The story continues with many other marvelous deeds that might seem more akin to a modern action movie. A statue broken by the demon-possessed is restored by the sprinkling of holy water; smoked fish hanging in a window are brought to life and seen swimming in water; Simon is beaten by the slaves of his former benefactor who also empty pots of filth on his head; a baby at the breast is given the gift of speech only to insult Simon as an abomination of God, and announce a showdown at the Forum on the coming Sabbath. Simon is then struck dumb and driving from the city until the appointed time. With the scene set for a final confrontation, Peter moves about Rome performing miracles and preaching. When Simon and Peter meet at the Forum before the assembled crowds they joust verbally before being given a test by a prefect who commands Simon to kill a man and Peter to raise him from the dead. Peter naturally passes the test by raising the young man. Another dead man to be raised is set before both

18. NTA 2.283.
19. NTA 2.290.

Peter and Simon. The one who fails the test will be burned alive. Simon was able to have the dead man raise his head, open his eyes, and bow toward Simon. But Peter makes the man rise wholly and completely, and thereupon urges the crowd not to burn Simon, for evil should not be repaid with evil.

Later in the story Peter and Simon face off once again, this time on the Via Sacra, leading to the Forum. Simon began to fly all over Rome, "passing over its temples and its hills."[20] Peter in turn prayed to Jesus that Simon would fall and be crippled, but not die. At that moment Simon fell from the sky and broke his leg in three places. The people stoned the maimed Simon and "from that time they all believed in Peter."[21]

The Acts of Peter then relates his martyrdom, precipitated by a certain prefect by the name of Agrippa whose wife, Xanthippe, was converted to Christianity and thereupon became a celibate. Agrippa, and many other men whose wives behaved similarly due to their new found faith, became enraged and had Peter arrested and crucified. Peter requests that he be crucified upside down (ch. 37) in the likeness of the first man, i.e., the upside-down (fallen) nature of humanity. Interestingly, Nero is told of Peter's death after the fact and censures Agrippa; for Nero wanted to punish Peter more severely. This is all in the Greek version of Acts of Peter.

In addition to the Greek, there is also a Latin version, which is longer than its Greek counterpart and dated later as well. The Latin version, also referred to as Pseudo-Linus *Martyrdom of Blessed Peter the Apostle*, includes more details than the Greek version, as its being longer than the Greek version suggests. The Latin work is attributed to Linus, the bishop of Rome who succeeded Peter; but that authorship is spurious, thus the "Pseudo-Linus." The date of the work is uncertain, but it is not earlier than 381 CE owing to its doctrinal expressions resembling the Council of Constantinople's theology of that same year.[22] And the latest date would be about the middle of the sixth century, to when the "Passion of the Saints Processus and Martinianus" is dated, as it is quoted by Pseudo-Linus.

Some of the many interesting details present in the Latin, but not found in the Greek include the names of Peter's prison guards, Processus and Martinianus, and the "Domine, quo vadis" story (though a different word is actually used rather than "vadis," but means the same thing). In that story, Peter flees the city of Rome only to meet Jesus, who is going to Rome.

20. *NTA* 2.312.
21. *NTA* 2.313.
22. Cf. Eastman *Ancient Martyrdom Accounts*, 28.

Peter asks Jesus, "Lord, where are you going?" (Domine, quo pergis?) to which Jesus replies, "I am going to Rome to be crucified again."[23]

Another interesting detail found in certain Latin version places the locale of Peter's crucifixion at the "place which is called naumachia next to the obelisk of Nero on the mountain. For there a cross had been placed."[24] A naumachia is a place where mock sea battles were staged. It can also refer to the battle itself. An arena would be flooded with water, at least a few feet deep, and small ships and boats would dart about in dramatic combat. One might think this juicy bit of information, combined with the obelisk of Nero on the mountain, would help us pinpoint the location the author had in mind. But there are several problematic elements with which to contend. Some readers, informed by modern popular thought and sensibilities, immediately call to mind the Vatican. Though there was at the time of Peter's martyrdom the circus of Gaius (Caligula) at the Vatican, and we know an obelisk stood nearby, that circus was not a naumachia. It seems placing the crucifixion of Peter at the Vatican is ruled out by this Latin text. And yet, the second-century emperor Trajan built a naumachia near Vatican Hill in about 109 CE. If this is the naumachia referred to by our Latin text, it would be an anachronism to say Peter was crucified at that naumachia, as Peter was crucified at least forty years earlier. So perhaps the author meant the Vatican, and meant to refer to the naumachia that was built by Trajan, but did not mean to suggest that the naumachia was there when Peter was crucified.

There were also many other obelisks besides the one at the Vatican in the city at the time Peter would have been martyred. Roman authors tell us that Nero built a naumachia at the Campus Martius (field of Mars). Today the Campo de' Fiori, Pantheon, and Piazza Navona are all situated where the ancient Campus Martius was. And there were obelisks there as well, and some still stand. But with such a large geographical territory with several possible obelisks, it is not clear precisely where in the Campus Martius the martyrdom might have been. So even though the Pseudo-Linus text claims that Peter was crucified at the "naumachia next to the obelisk of Nero on the mountain," there is no certainty as to where that was, or to which place the author is referring.

---

23. Pseudo-Linus, *Martyrdom of Blessed Peter the Apostle* in Eastman, *Ancient Martyrdom Accounts*, 42.

24. "*ad locum qui uocatur Naumachiae iuxta obeliscum Neronis in montem. illic enim crux posita erat*" (Pseudo-Linus, *Martyrdom of Blessed Peter the Apostle* in Eastman *Ancient Martyrdom Accounts*, 48–49).

There is another even later legend, sometimes attributed to an obscure version of the Acts of Peter, but more properly attested in the eigteenth-century *Acta Sanctorum*, which says that Peter was crucified *inter duas metas*,[25] "between two metae." It is first attested in writing by Flavio Biondo, though he admits the location is unclear.[26] We will discuss that legend in more detail below.

Perhaps it is easy for us to see why the earliest edition of the Acts of Peter was not considered canonical or inspired, as it reads more like "fan fiction" today. There is little if any historically reliable data in the story, but it becomes popular in legend and lore, and is therefore significant for our understanding of certain Roman sites.

Acts of Paul

Like the Acts of Peter, the Acts of Paul is dated to the late second century, for it is referred to by Tertullian in about the year 200. The Acts of Paul is also significant for some in that it gives us a physical description of the apostle: "A man small of stature, with a bald head and crooked legs, in a good state of body, with eyebrows meeting and nose somewhat hooked, full of friendliness; for now he appeared like a man, and now he had the face of an angel."[27] Though it would be difficult to say that the description matches the historical Paul, we will see that this passage informs artistic depictions of Paul throughout the city, especially his scanty hair.

There are different parts that make up the Acts of Paul, including two main stories: "Acts of Paul and Thecla," and "the Martyrdom of the Holy Apostle Paul." It was precisely the Acts of Paul and Thecla to which Tertullian objected for the document presented the woman Thecla preaching and baptizing, even if it was she herself that she baptized! Tertullian writes, "But if the writings which wrongly go under Paul's name, claim Thecla's example as a licence for women's teaching and baptizing, let them know that, in Asia, the presbyter who composed that writing, as if he were augmenting Paul's

---

25. *AS*, Junii, VII.2.2 53–54. See http://acta.chadwyck.com/all/fulltext?ACTION=by offset&WARN=N&OFFSET=39892648&DIV=0&FILE=../session/1467227155_15796.

26. "Nam cum ad terebinthum, inter duas metas, illum fuisse passum constans sit fama, quis sit is locus omnino ignoratur" (Biondo, *De Roma Instaurata*, in Valentini and Zucchetti, *Codice topografico della città di Roma*, 4:272).

27. Acts of Paul and Thecla 2. *NTA* 2.239.

fame from his own store, after being convicted, and confessing that he had done it from love of Paul, was removed from his office."[28]

The other main section of the Acts of Paul, "the Martyrdom of the Holy Apostle Paul," tells how Paul came to Rome preaching the good news, where Titus and Luke were waiting for him. Some even from Caesar's household came to him. In a story reminiscent of the raising of Eutychus (Acts 20:7–12), one evening Nero's cup-bearer Patroclus sat on a high window listening to Paul before falling to his death. Like the case with Eutychus who suffered a similar fall that resulted in death, Paul raised Patroclus, but not before Nero heard that his cup-bearer had died. When Patroclus presented himself alive to Nero and attributed it to the power of Christ, king of the ages, Nero became angry. Even more, Nero learned that other soldiers in his service also counted themselves as Christians. As Nero considered himself king of the ages, he imprisoned the self-identified Christian soldiers and thus began his persecution of other Christians, in which Paul was caught up. Nero sentenced Paul to beheading, but not before hearing his case personally. After hearing from Paul, Nero reconfirmed his decision to have Paul beheaded, to which Paul responded that he would arise and appear alive to Nero, proving that he [Paul] lives in Christ Jesus who is coming to judge the world. The executioner wielded the sword and upon severing Paul's head milk spurted upon the soldier's clothing, which was taken to be a sign of God's glory. As promised, Paul appeared before Nero alive, predicting that Nero would face many evils and punishments due to his unjust punishment of Paul.[29]

A later, fourth–fifth-century legendary Latin account, the "Passio Sancti Pauli Apostoli" (The Passion of Saint Paul the Apostle), relates how a follower of Paul by the name of Plautilla gave him her scarf by which he blindfolded his eyes before his execution. Immediately following the execution the scarf could not be found. Plautilla is later said to have the bloodstained scarf.[30] This scene will be the source for many images and icons we shall see in the city, including on the door of St. Paul Outside the Walls, and the Filarete Door at St. Peter's.

Much later legend associates Paul's house arrest at San Paolo alla Regola in Rome (see chapter below) or Santa Maria in Via Lata (see below). The name of the village where the University of Dallas Rome campus

---

28. Tertullian, *On Baptism*, 17.
29. For more on the Acts of Paul, see *NTA* 2.213–270.
30. Tajra, *Martyrdom of St. Paul*, 142.

is located (near modern day Frattochie) bears the name attesting to Peter and Paul's presence there: Due Santi (Two Saints). The village is on the Via Appia, the very road Paul took into Rome according to Acts of the Apostles. Legend has it that Peter went out to meet Paul. As Paul approached Rome on the Appia way, Peter went out to meet him. His encounter took place at Due Santi. Of course, there are many more, countless legends, referring to Peter and Paul in Rome. Historically most of these (if not all) are circumspect, but as the Italians say, *Se non è vero, è ben trovato* (Even if it's not true, it's a good story).

Despite the paucity of historical information, an immense liturgical and theological edifice was constructed upon the traditions of Peter and Paul's presence in Rome and their martyrdom therein. In the middles ages it seems some legends were lost as new stories emerged. By the time of the Renaissance the place of Peter's martyrdom was thought to have been on the Janiculum (Gianicolo), the Mons Aureus, "golden mountain," Thus in 1502 Bramante erected the Tempietto (the little temple), a master piece of Renaissance architecture over the place where Peter was to have been crucified. In fact, Bramante built the Tempietto over a ninth-century church. Today the Tempietto is situated in the cloister to the right of San Pietro in Montorio (Montorio being a corruption of Mons Aureus, named so because of the yellow sand on the top of this hill in antiquity).

Acts of Peter and Paul

This later work (ca. 450–550 CE) gives information similar to that of other stories. Like the Acts of Peter and the Acts of Paul, the Acts of Peter and Paul has a bifurcated textual history. We have a Latin and a Greek version, with the latter being longer. Still, much of the general story of the Acts of Peter and Paul is based on the earlier works. Some Latin manuscripts end with "I, Marcellus, have written what I saw."[31] The Marcellus in this case would be the disciple of Simon Magus who later converted to orthodox Christianity. Since that attribution would be a clear anachronism, the Latin work is often titled, Pseudo-Marcellus, *Passion and Acts of the Holy Apostles Peter and Paul*, and abbreviated as *Passio*.[32]

---

31. Eastman, *Ancient Martyrdom Accounts*, 224.

32. The *Passio Sanctorum Apostolorum Petri et Pauli* "The Passion of the Holy Apostles Peter and Paul," is the Latin recension of the Greek *Martyrion* or "The Martyrdom of the Holy Apostles Peter and Paul" (Tajra, *Martyrdom of St. Paul*, 143).

The Passio chapter 59, as the Acts of Paul chapter 59, state simply that that "Paul was decapitated on the Ostian Road."[33] In the Greek *Acts of Peter and Paul* 80, the story is expanded to:

> The sentence having been handed down, Peter and Paul were removed from Nero's presence. Paul was led, chained, to the place where he was to be decapitated, three miles from the City, by an escort of three soldiers of noble blood.
>
> When they were about an arrow's flight from the city gate, there came to them a pious woman who, when she saw Paul in chains, was greatly moved and burst into tears. The woman's name was Perpetua and she had only one eye. Seeing her weeping, Paul said to her: "Give me your scarf and at my return I shall give it back to you." She took her scarf and immediately gave it to him. The soldiers approached the woman and said to her: "Woman, why do you wish to lose your scarf? Do you not know that he is on his way to be decapitated?" But Perpetua answered them: "I beseech you, by Caesar's sword, to cover his eyes with this scarf when you behead him." And so it was.
>
> They beheaded him at the demesne of the Aquae Salviae, near the pine-tree. According to God's will, before the soldiers returned, the scarf, soaked with blood, was restituted to the woman and as soon as she put it on, her eye was suddenly opened.[34]

Later, in chapter 87 of the same work, the reader is told that there was an attempt to steal the bodies of Peter and Paul so they were interred temporarily at the Catacombs on the Via Appia (San Sebastiano).[35]

Thus in this work we see a clear development as to the place of martyrdom for Paul. In both the Acts of Paul (59) and the *Passio* (59), and even the *Liber Pontificalis* (22, as we shall see below) the place of Paul's death was the via Ostiense. Now, in this sixth-century work, the Greek version of the *Acts of Peter and Paul*, we have a new location introduced, the Aquae Salviae heretofore never mentioned in the traditional and legendary material about Paul's death. We will explore this in more detail in the section below on the Abbey of the Three Fountains at Aquae Salviae.

---

33. Eastman, *Ancient Martyrdom Accounts*, 265.

34. From Tajra, *Martyrdom of St. Paul*, 148–49. For another modern translation, see Eastman, *Ancient Martyrdom Accounts*, 307.

35. Tajra, *Martyrdom of St. Paul*, 149.

Catalogus Liberianus

From 354 CE we have the *Catalogus Liberianus* (*Liberian Catalog*, abbreviated as *CL*) which lists all of the Popes up to the then current Pope Liberius, who died in 366 CE. This text was not composed in its entirety in 354, but drew on earlier works. So, it can be difficult to determine with certainty the sources used by the *CL* and any redactions. There are a number of oddities in the work, many of which have to do with Peter. The *CL* claims that Peter was the founder of the church at Rome and served for 25 years, one month, and nine days, and that he took up this episcopate after Jesus' ascension. But even Acts of the Apostles tells us that Peter was exercising a ministry in Jerusalem after the ascension. When would he have gone to Rome? There is a cryptic phrase in Acts 12:17 that says Peter departed Jerusalem "for another place." Some have understood that to mean Rome, and by so doing, they are able to account for Peter's presence there. Still, as we noted above, when Paul wrote his Letter to the Romans, Peter is never mentioned, even among the numerous believers Paul names in Romans 16. But the *Catalogus Liberianus* says Peter was the founder of the church in Rome, a phrase that can be understood to say that Peter was simply exercising his episcopacy for twenty-five years, one month, and nine days, without being in Rome that entire time.

A further challenge is presented when the *CL* attests to Peter's death along with Paul on the third day before the Kalends (first day of the month) of July during the reign of Nero (June 29). Problematic also is the dating presented by the *CL*, which would make Peter's episcopacy last from about 30–55 CE. As we noted above, it seems likely that Peter would have been martyred during the persecution of Nero after the great fire of Rome, not a decade earlier. For our purposes, a significant piece of information we glean from this work is the twenty-five-year episcopacy of Peter, as well as the site of his burial "at the catacombs."[36] This twenty-five-year Petrine ministry will set a standard of sorts, growing into a legend we will see at St. Peter's that no pope would ever serve longer than Peter. Yet, it should be noted, that this length of service in the Petrine see has been overcome by very few popes, and only fairly recently.

---

36. Davis, *Book of Pontiffs*, 93.

Liber Pontificalis

The *Catalogus Liberianus* formed the basis of a later work known as the *Liber Pontificalis*, (*Book of Pontiffs*, abbreviated as *LP*) which lists and discusses 108 lives of the Popes up to the year 870. The *LP* supplemented information found in the *CL* but often the "new" data was invented or imagined. Scholars debate the date of this compilation. Certainly, the final edition was done in the ninth century, but there were likely earlier editions. Davis argues in favor of a sixth-century edition, "produced no later than the 540s."[37] It is the nature of such lists and biographies that one or another scribe can continue to add to them, updating them to then current events. But our purpose with the *LP* is not to delve into the early Middle Ages, but to explore the basis of legends regarding Peter, Paul, and the early church. So we can follow Davis in considering the material about that time period to have been compiled and edited in the first half of the sixth century.

It is significant that *LP* adds to the material in *CL* about Peter. In particular, it clarifies that Peter's episcopacy in Rome was twenty-five years, two months, and three days, following a seven year episcopacy in Antioch. It also states that "he was crowned with martyrdom along with Paul in the 38th year after the Lord suffered. He was buried on the Via Aurelia at the temple of Apollo, close to the place where he was crucified, and to Nero's palace on the Vatican, and to the Triumphal territory, on 29 June."[38]

Many of the geographical markers named by the *LP* seem mixed up. For example, in reality the Via Aurelia crossed the Tiber just south of Tiber Island (see map on page 22). From there it went west out of the city south of the Ager Vaticanus and near the Janiculum Hill. But, the temple of Apollo, dedicated by Augustus, was near the Circus Maximus. And neither the Via Aurelia nor the temple of Apollo seems close to the Vatican, where Nero had gardens rather than a palace. So the *LP* gives us pause in considering how much information was really known in the sixth century about the burial place of Peter. Of course, by that time the Basilica of St. Peter had been built two hundred years prior, but there is no mention of that marking Peter's burial site. Instead, the *LP* continues its review of pontiffs with Linus and Cletus. Both are said to have been buried, "close to St. Peter's body on the Vatican."[39] So whatever *LP* meant to preserve with the traditions about

---

37. Ibid., iii.
38. Ibid., 2.
39. Ibid.

the Via Aurelia, etc., it's clear that *LP* considers St. Peter to have been buried at the Vatican.

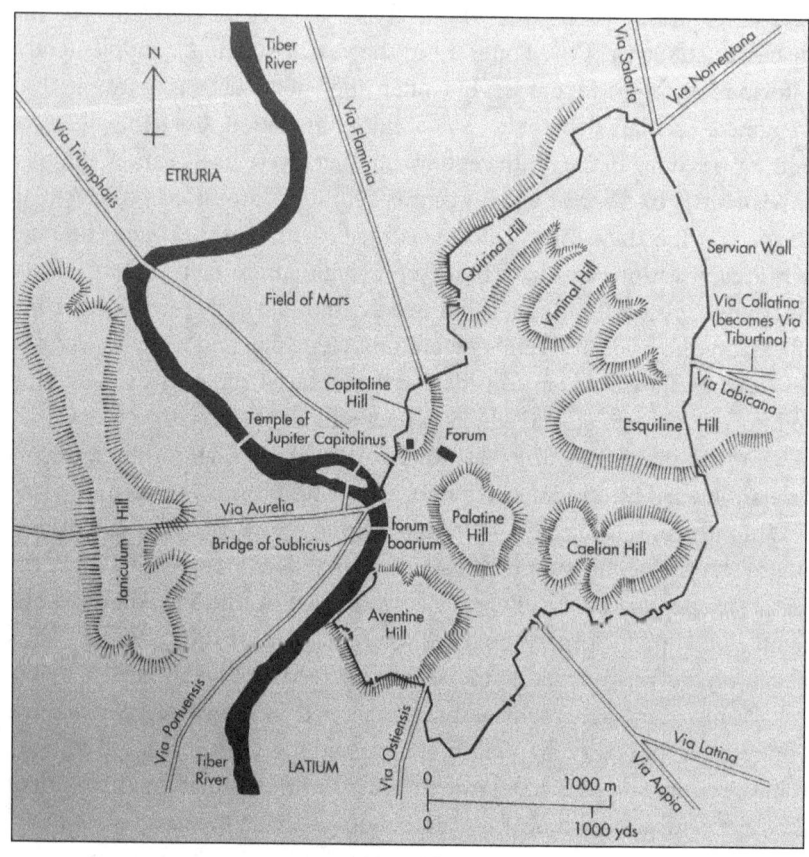

Plan of early Rome with the Seven Hills and the Servian Wall.

Mirabilia Urbis Romae

The *Mirabilia Urbis Romae* (*Wonders of the City of Rome*) is a medieval guidebook to the city of Rome that was written about 1140. The book was considered authoritative and reliable for centuries, until Renaissance scholars began to question some of its fanciful claims. The work is now considered a guidebook more informed by imagination and inventiveness than historical knowledge. Still, it informs our understanding of the medieval period and the many fantastical claims about the places and people of Rome. Though the *Mirabilia* is dated to the twelfth century, there is another fourteenth-century manuscript known as the *Mirabiliana* that has at least one legend that will inform our visit to St. Paul's at Tre Fontane.

Golden Legend

A medieval best-seller, there are more than 1000 copies of the *Legenda Aurea* (*Golden Legend*) book still intact. It was compiled by Jacobus de Voragine in the 1260s from existing material and intended for preachers and others who could use vignettes to illustrate their orations. His book owes its (commercial) success to the newly founded Dominicans who used it extensively in their travels, as Jacobus drew on some earlier material compiled by Dominicans themselves. It was called "golden" as it was considered worth its weight in gold; it was *legenda*, not in the sense of "made up fairy tale," but in the Latin sense of the word, "(meant) to be read aloud."[40] For our purposes, the *Golden Legend* preserves the story of Peter and Paul coming to Constantine in a dream, the result of which is the construction of St. Peter's Basilica. It also gives us the name of Longinus, the Roman soldier who pierced Jesus' corpse with a lance.

De Roma Instaurata

The three-volume work by Flavio Biondo (*Rome Restored* [1444–1448]) continues to be a valuable source of information today. The humanist Biondo has been called one of the first archaeologists, and it was he as well as some others who questioned the reliability of the *Mirabilia*. For example, he is the first to record in writing the legend of Peter being crucified "inter duas metas" and at the same time admits he does not know where that location would be.[41] In the ruins of Rome covered in fields he reimagined the glory of the city in its prime. The work is essentially a reconstruction of ancient Rome using the best scholarly knowledge of the day, much of it done first hand by Biondo himself. He is such an important figure for the city that we can see Biondo's funeral monument in the floor of Santa Maria in Aracoeli.

---

40. De Voragine and Ryan, *Golden Legend*, xi–xii.
41. See footnote 26.

Sanctuarium seu Vitae Sanctorum

Bonino Mombrizio (1424-ca. 1500) assembled and published a work on hagiography in about 1480. The work was edited and republished in two volumes in 1910. For our purposes, this work is important in that it preserves the legend of the martyrdom of Saints Processus and Martinianus.

Acta Sanctorum

The *Acta Sanctorum* (*Acts of the Saints,* abbreviated as *AS*) is a late work from the post-Renaissance period. It could even be said that the volumes were not completed until 1940! Begun by a Jesuit, Heribert Rosweyde (1569–1629), the work was continued and expanded by his Jesuit confrere Jean Bolland (1596–1665). Bolland completed five volumes and inspired a movement of others, who took the name the Bollandists, and they sustained the work. By the time the Jesuits were suppressed in the eigteenth century about 50 volumes had been written, following the calendar of saints' days in the Roman liturgy. The work is significant for a number of reasons, not least of which is the introduction of the historical-critical method to the lives of the saints. Even so, AS preserves much legendary material.

It is in the *AS* that we have a positive identification of Peter being crucified *inter duas metas* (between two metas). The *AS* is here preserving a medieval legend that formed the basis of Bramante's Tempietto on the Janiculum (see San Pietro in Montorio).

A meta is the Latin term for "cone," sometimes in a pyramidal shape, other times resembling an obelisk or a modern-day Halloween witch's hat. A meta was often used as a marker in the city, or as a marker that indicated the end of a circus race track. During the Renaissance, scholars interpreted the two metae in this obscure version of the text to be the Meta of Remus (now known as the Pyramide, or the tomb of Gaius Cestius)[42] and the Meta of Romulus (near the Vatican). The location of San Pietro in Montorio was the point between these two metae (see notes for that church below).

---

42. The pyramidal tomb of Gaius Cestius was known in the Middle Ages and into the Renaissance as the Meta of Remus. It was thought to be the burial place of Remus. A Meta of Romulus, thought to be his burial place, was near the Vatican, adjacent to the Mausoleum of Hadrian (Castel San'Angelo). Unfortunately, no trace of the Meta of Romulus exists today as it was partially destroyed in 1499 (to widen a street) and finally destroyed in 1564 for the relocation and building of Santa Maria in Traspontina.

2

Brief History of First-Century Rome

How did a religion founded on the teachings and actions of a backwater first-century Aramaic-speaking Jewish carpenter become a global force with more than one billion members of a church that claims Latin as its official language, and Greek as the language of its founding documents (the New Testament)? Part of the answer lies in first-century Rome, the capital of the cultural and military empire of the Mediterranean world. It can be difficult for modern people to appreciate the many obstacles the early church overcame. Perhaps we can use an analogy.

Suppose a Mayan woodworker from Guatemala, speaking his native Mayan language, began a movement which was punctuated by his violent and public death at the hands of the Guatemalan government. Not long after, his followers claimed he was no longer dead but had risen. In order to spread this message to a larger audience in Central America and even Mexico they wrote their stories in Spanish, a language the Mayan woodworker did not even speak. In a matter of decades these Spanish-speaking people and their stories found their way to the U.S., even to the capital city, Washington, D.C. where some of the movement's leaders settled.

Many well-educated English-speaking peoples in the U.S. would dismiss such a fanciful tale of a resurrected Mayan, whose movement seemed to resemble a cult. Yet this small, marginalized community continued to read the sacred stories written in Spanish about their Mayan founder. They attracted some of the poorer, lower class, and less well-educated English-speakers to their movement but not much more. To extend our analogy further, if we fast forward three centuries we could see that this small community had become dominated by English-speakers, the language of the

U.S. with its cultural and military empire. Their sacred texts were translated from the Spanish original into English, making it another step removed from its Mayan founder's language. Though it may seem far-fetched, suppose further that the U.S. was crushed under the weight of its own hubris and consumption, and ultimately collapsed as a social order. The now English speaking Mayan sect stepped in and offered support services. It was one of only a few remaining vestiges of social order. And from the ashes of U.S. civilization the Mayan sect rose like a phoenix and became dominant.

Of course, this is only a fanciful imaginative exercise, and seems wildly beyond the realm of possibility. By way of analogy it expresses what a first-century Roman audience might have thought of a similar story, the Christian story. In the first century, the Roman Empire and the city of Rome itself was dominant throughout the known world. There was little to stand in its way; and those who did were crushed utterly and severely. No "superstitious cult" (as one Roman author referred to Christianity) would take the place of this dominant cultural force. And yet, in a matter of centuries that is precisely what happened. To better place ourselves in this context of first-century Rome, we will briefly review some highlights of the period.

The City of Rome

According to legend, Rome was founded in 753 BCE on the banks of the Tiber, in a valley surrounded by seven hills. Over the course of many centuries, first under the seven kings (753–509 BCE), and then under the Republic (509–27 BCE), the city grew to include the Campus Martius (Field of Mars), Tiber Island, and the area across the Tiber, known today as Trastevere. Rome in the first century was a city of nearly one million people, including about 50,000 Jews. The ancient city built on seven hills city had grown beyond those once natural borders to a size of about five square miles that was divided into fourteen districts.

The First Emperors

Though it is obvious and therefore sounds strange to say it, the Roman world did not change its calendar from 1 BCE to 1 CE when Jesus was born. Of course, it was only centuries later that Christians developed the calendar based not on the founding of the city of Rome (753 BCE) but on the birth of Jesus. Unfortunately, the monk who was primarily responsible for performing this task made some minor errors so that scholars today would claim that Jesus was actually born around 7 or 6 BCE. Even so, the system of counting years has now become so standard and pervasive (at least in the West), that there is no real impetus to "fix" it so that it might more accurately reflect the years since Jesus' birth. As a result, this monk can be thought of as the first millennial bug!

Octavian/Augustus (27 BCE–14 CE)

Octavian (b. 63 BCE–14 CE) was the great nephew, adopted son and heir of Julius Caesar. Jesus was born during the reign of Octavian, also known as Augustus (r. 27 BCE– 14 CE). Though he referred to himself as "first among the citizens" (*princeps civitatis*) rather than an emperor, it was his policies and length of service that truly disengaged Rome from its republican moorings and initiated the age of the Roman Empire. Octavian initially did this by allying with two others, Mark Antony and Mark Lepidus, to form a triumvirate (three men) which among other things avenged the death of Octavian's uncle, Julius Caesar. The triumvirate was established by law and ruled the empire briefly (two five-year terms, from 44–34 BCE) before its members turned on one another. When the bloodshed subsided Octavian was declared *Augustus* (revered) by the Senate and he eventually dedicated an Altar of Peace, which can still be seen today on the banks of the Tiber. Octavian dedicated himself to improving the administration of the empire, reforming the army, and building projects in Rome among many other notable achievements. Of Rome, Octavian said he found a city of sun-dried brick and left a city of marble.[1]

Octavian's strongest ally throughout this period was his childhood friend and military genius Marcus Agrippa. As a "reward" for his loyalty and friendship, Octavian gave Agrippa his daughter Julia in marriage, thereby making him his son-in-law. This marriage produced at least five children, including Agrippina the elder, mother of the emperor Caligula.

Octavian knew King Herod, the same Herod who in Matthew's Gospel is said to have massacred the innocents. This Herod ("the Great") had such a reputation for ruthlessness, even killing many members of his own family, that Octavian, learning that Herod had killed his son Antipater, quipped that he would rather be Herod's pig (*hus*) than his son (*huios*).[2]

1. Suetonius, *Augustus* 28, in *Lives of the Caesars*.
2. Macrobius, *Saturnalia* 2.4.11. (The pun is Greek rather than Latin.)

Herod the Great died in 4 BCE and Octavian divided his kingdom between his three sons: Archelaus ruled over Judea, Samaria, and Idumea; Herod Antipas ruled over Galilee and Peraea; and Philip ruled over Gaulanitis. This arrangement lasted for about ten years and was considered by the Romans to be a complete failure. So in 6 CE Octavian made Judea into an imperial (rather than senatorial) province ruled directly by Rome. Herod Antipas and Philip were allowed to rule over their smaller regions.

In 12 BCE Octavian's childhood friend, close ally, and son-in-law Marcus Agrippa died while on campaign. His death sent Octavian into mourning for a month. Octavian was a few weeks shy of his 77th birthday, a remarkable feat for the ancient world, before he died and left the empire to his adopted son and heir, Tiberius, who reigned from 14–37 CE.

Tiberius (14–37)

Tiberius was a conquering general whose mother had divorced his father and married Octavian, making Tiberius his stepson, and eventual heir. According to Josephus, Tiberius expelled all the Jews from Rome in 19 CE. He also conscripted four thousand of these for military service, sending them to the island of Sardinia (Ant. 18.3.5; 83–84). In the year 20, Herod Antipas in a move to curry favor with the emperor founded a new capital of Galilee and called it Tiberias. The town, on the coast of the Sea of Galilee, grew to be so prominent that the body of water itself became known as the Sea of Tiberias.

It was also during Tiberius' reign that Jesus was crucified. Shortly thereafter but in no way related, a delegation from Judea/Syria went to Rome to lodge a complaint against the cruel practices of Pontius Pilate, who had been prefect of Judea since 26 CE. For example Pilate attempted to have images of Tiberius installed in the Temple, against the wishes of the Jewish people and Mosaic Law. Later, he took money meant for the Temple and used it to construct an aqueduct. When the people protested he authorized the Roman soldiers to kill members of the populace at will under the guise of stemming an insurrection (Josephus, *Antiquities*. 18.3.1–2). Apparently Tiberius took the complaints with some seriousness for he recalled Pilate, who made his way to Rome. But before Pilate arrived, Tiberius died on March 16, 37 CE. The resulting power vacuum or "interregnum" in Judea is the likely time when Stephen would have been stoned to death (Acts 6).

BRIEF HISTORY OF FIRST-CENTURY ROME

Caligula (37–41)

After the death of Tiberius, his grand-nephew, and adopted grandson Gaius, son of the victorious General Germanicus and Agrippina the elder, became emperor. As a young boy Gaius was known by the nickname, "little boots," or "bootikins," (*Caligula*) as he used to march around the army camps with his father in army boots, issuing orders to the soldiers, who gave him the name. The name remained throughout his adult life, though few would call him that to his face. Caligula was a despot and stories of his madness are myriad including his desire to make his horse a consul (high ranking official) and his desire to erect a statue of himself in the Jerusalem Temple. Interestingly, in 39 CE Herod Antipas petitioned Gaius to be made king, but was also accused by his nephew, Herod Agrippa, of treason against the new emperor. Rather than name Antipas a king, Caligula exiled him, and effectively gave his kingdom to Herod Agrippa. Despite this ignoble end, it should be noted that Antipas was the second longest reigning Herodian ever (4 BCE–39 CE), which speaks to his otherwise sophisticated political and administrative skill. Caligula's own short reign ended in 41 CE as he was the first of many emperors to be assassinated. Immediately after the assassination, the Praetorian Guard (Rome's elite forces that functioned as a body guard for the emperor) found Caligula's uncle, Claudius, the brother of Germanicus, hiding behind a curtain, perhaps fearing for his life. The guard named him emperor.

Claudius (41–54)

Claudius, born in 10 BCE, reigned from 41–54 CE. He was helped to the throne by Herod Agrippa who was also born in 10 BCE, as the grandson of Herod the Great. Herod Agrippa, named after Marcus Agrippa, was educated in Rome where he met and developed close relations with members of the imperial family, not least of which was Caligula and Claudius. His connections saved Jerusalem from many potential flash points, including Caligula's plan to erect a statue of himself in the Jerusalem Temple. Deft diplomacy prevented this certain catastrophe. Still, this Herod Agrippa is the same Herod who persecuted the church in Jerusalem (Acts 12:1–23) which resulted in the martyrdom of James.

When Herod Agrippa died in 44 CE, he left an heir (Herod Agrippa II, born in 28 CE) too young to take the kingdom. So Claudius named a

Roman governor to oversee the kingdom Agrippa left behind. This young Herod Agrippa II was in Rome at the time of his father's death, and stayed there to be educated like his father, enjoying Claudius' court. When he came of age, Agrippa II returned to Judea. It is this Herod and his sister Berenice who heard Paul's defense prior to his journey to Rome, as recounted in Acts 25:13—26:32. We will return to their story below in the tumultuous decade of the 60s.

For his part, Claudius was an effective administrator. Two seemingly minor matters of his administration are important for our consideration. According the later historian Cassius Dio (ca. 155–235 CE) in the first year of his reign Claudius forbid the Jews in the city from meeting (60.6.6). Cassius says that Claudius would have driven them out of the city, but their numbers would have made that task troublesome. But it seems that later in Claudius' reign the cost of enforcing such an order was more palatable for the Roman historian Suetonius tells us that Claudius' patience wore thin and in 49 CE he in fact did drive out all Jews from the city as they "were making constant disturbances at the instigation of *Chrēstus*" (Suetonius, *Life of Claudius*, 25.4, in *Lives of the Caesars*). The Greek name *Chrēstus*, meaning "good, useful" was a common slave name. Its pronunciation was the same as the Greek term, *Christos*, meaning "anointed," which itself is a translation of the Hebrew term, "messiah." In 49 CE *Christos* was not a popular name, though *Chrēstus* was. Suetonius, a well-educated Roman, naturally thinks the argument was about a person named *Chrēstus*. But with our benefit of hindsight, it seems that someone overheard arguments between Jews and Jewish Christians over the person and meaning of the Christ, i.e., the Messiah. And this would have been a theological argument that would not have been on Suetonius' radar. He interpreted it in the most common sense way possible. Jews were making constant disturbances at the instigation of someone named *Chrēstus*. So in 41 CE Jews were forbidden from meeting in the city, and by 49 CE they were expelled altogether. These two minor administrative matters, mentioned casually by different biographers, shed light on the development of Christianity in the city of Rome.

We even know the names of some of those Jewish Christians who were exiled from Rome as Luke tells us in Acts:

> After this he [Paul] left Athens and went to Corinth. There he met a Jew named Aquila, a native of Pontus, who had recently come from Italy with his wife Priscilla because Claudius had ordered all the Jews to leave Rome. He went to visit them and, because he

practiced the same trade, stayed with them and worked, for they were tentmakers by trade (Acts 18:1–3).

It was also during the reign of Claudius, about the year 50, that a Roman soldier exposed himself in the Jerusalem Temple! The Roman commander Cumanus had placed guards in the Temple portico to prevent any uprising during the Passover celebration. It was on the fourth day of this celebration one of the Roman soldiers exposed his bare genitals to the crowd, which erupted with fury. They protested to Cumanus who simply outfitted the soldiers in full battle gear and placed them at the fortress overlooking the Temple. This caused the crowds to become so fearful they created a stampede, killing and crushing thousands in their desperate flight to escape.[3]

But returning to imperial drama and politics, eventually Claudius married his own niece, Agrippina the younger, as his fourth wife; it was her third marriage. Agrippina was a great granddaughter of Augustus, and a sister of Caligula. Her parents were Agrippina the elder and Germanicus. This marriage was considered incestuous by Roman custom and required Senate approval. Agrippina brought a son from a prior marriage to her imperial nuptials with Claudius. The son's name was Nero, whom she convinced Claudius to adopt as heir. When Claudius seemed to repent of having made that decision Agrippina made her move and assassinated the 63-year-old Claudius with poisoned mushrooms in 54 CE.

The death of Claudius meant the end to the Jewish exile from Rome, so Priscilla (a diminutive nickname for Prisca), Aquila, and other Jews would have returned to the city. By the time Paul writes to the Romans in the winter of 57–58 he greets the couple by name (Rom 16:3–5a): "Greet Prisca and Aquila, my co-workers in Christ Jesus, who risked their necks for my life, to whom not only I am grateful but also all the churches of the Gentiles; greet also the church at their house" (NABRE). With the five-year Jewish exile from Rome over, Jewish Christians would have returned to a church/churches that were Gentile Christian and presumably were more progressive in their thinking about issues such as dietary restrictions and other matters related to Mosaic Law. Perhaps this friction is the source of the differences between the "strong and weak" that Paul addresses in Rom 14.

---

3. Cf. Josephus, *Ant.* 20.5.3, 106; Josephus, *War* 2.12.1, 224.

Nero (54–67): The First Five Years (54–59)

The period 54–59 was the most peaceful the Empire had seen. Nero was seventeen years old when he took the throne and seemed content to leave most imperial matters to his mother, Agrippina. Or perhaps it was the other way around as Agrippina was happy to placate Nero with women, wine, and song. Recall that Agrippina, as great granddaughter of Augustus had lived her life in the imperial court. She was at the center of power during the reign of Claudius, having been named "Augusta." After Claudius' death, she was named a priestess of his cult and so was able to attend meetings of the Senate. She was a strong woman who also wrote an autobiography, which unfortunately did not survive. She and her son Nero soon came to see each other as competitors.

We mentioned above that the edict barring Jews from the city that Claudius issued ended with his reign. Jewish Christians, including Prisca and Aquila, would have returned to Rome after a five-year hiatus when Gentile Christians, perhaps more libertine in their thinking with respect to Mosaic Law, had been the only Christian presence in the city. It was during this rather peaceful period of 54–59 that Paul would have written his letter to the Romans advising them to cooperate with authorities.

Nero eventually had ideas of his own about the administration of the empire that were being thwarted by his mother. As a result, he tried several times (unsuccessfully) to have her killed surreptitiously before finally sending in a squad to strike her through with a sword. She was assassinated in 59. So was the madness of Nero, who was able to rule now without his mother's interference.

The Turbulent Decade of the 60s

The decade of the 60s was to be punctuated with violence, fire, calamity, insurrection, martyrdoms, assassinations, struggle for power, and more. The empire had not seen anything like it and for the early Christians it might have seemed that the end-times were near.

Though there were many significant events in this decade that contributed to the sense of impending doom, four stand out as especially important for our purposes: (1) The young adult, now motherless, Nero continued to persecute his enemies, those of senatorial rank and many others; (2) The Great Fire of Rome; (3) the Jewish Insurrection and Destruction of the Temple; and (4) the year of the Four Emperors.

Nero (54–67): The Motherless Years (60–67)

With Agrippina out of the picture, and as a twenty-one-year-old man, Nero had sole, undisputed power over the greatest empire the world had seen. He thus began to systematically execute anyone whom he suspected of standing in his way, or usurping his power. Even Seneca, his tutor who functioned in a way that might call "prime minister," asked for permission to retire, but was compelled to commit suicide.[4] Nero murdered his own aunt Domitia, and according to Suetonius Nero kicked to death his second wife Poppea while she was pregnant. Suetonius also tells us that Nero, "resolved on the death of all the eminent men of the State . . . The children of those who were condemned were banished or put to death by poison or starvation; a number are known to have been slain all together at a single meal along with their preceptors and attendants, while others were prevented from earning their daily bread. After this he showed neither discrimination nor moderation in putting to death whomsoever he pleased on any pretext whatever."[5]

Nero also fancied himself an artist, composing verse and playing the lyre. In fact, during some performances he locked the doors, ensuring no one could leave. There are stories of women giving birth and men feigning death as the only way to leave the performance (Suetonius, *Nero*, 23, in *Lives of the Caesars*). He even introduced a musical contest into the Olympic games in Greece, a place where he received prizes for his lute-playing. This adulation caused him to say that, "the Greeks were the only ones who had an ear for music and that they alone were worthy of his efforts."[6] His love of the lyre would lead to one of the most popular legendary tales about him, that he fiddled while Rome burned.

---

4. Seneca's brother was Gallio, who was consul in Achaia, headquartered in Corinth. He heard Paul's case (Acts 18:12–17) when charges were brought against him by some Jewish leaders. Gallio essentially dismissed the matter against Paul.

5. Suetonius, *Nero*, 36–37, in *Lives of the Caesars*.

6. Ibid., 22.

THE ROME OF PETER AND PAUL—PART I

The Great Fire of Rome

Rome has been no stranger to devastation caused by fire. The crowded city, wooden structures, jammed quarters, narrow streets, and even unsafe cooking techniques led to fires in the city from time to time. It seems however that the fire of 64 was seared in the memory of both Romans and Christians alike.

According to the Roman historian Tacitus (ca. 55–ca. 120 CE), on July 19, 64 a great fire spread through the city of Rome, completely destroying most of the empire's capital. He describes the event in his *Annals*:

> There followed a disaster, whether due to chance or to the malice of the sovereign is uncertain—for each version has its sponsors—but graver and more terrible than any other which has befallen this city by the ravages of fire ... The flames, which in full career overran the level districts first, then shot up to the heights, and sank again to harry the lower parts, kept ahead of all remedial measures, the mischief travelling fast, and the town being an easy prey owing to the narrow, twisting lanes and formless streets typical of old Rome. In addition, shrieking and terrified women; fugitives stricken or immature in years; men consulting their own safety or the safety of others, as they dragged the infirm along or paused to wait for them, combined by their dilatoriness or their haste to impede everything. Often, while they glanced back to the rear, they were attacked on the flanks or in front; or, if they had made their escape into a neighbouring quarter, that also was involved in the flames, and even districts which they had believed remote from danger were found to be in the same plight. At last, irresolute what to avoid or what to seek, they crowded into the roads or threw themselves down in the fields: some who had lost the whole of their means—their daily bread included—chose to die, though the way of escape was open, and were followed by others, through love for the relatives whom they had proved unable to rescue ...
>
> Nero, who at the time was staying in Antium, did not return to the capital until the fire was nearing the house by which he had connected the Palatine with the Gardens of Maecenas. It proved impossible, however, to stop it from engulfing both the Palatine and the house and all their surroundings. Still, as a relief to the homeless and fugitive populace, he opened the Campus Martius, the buildings of Agrippa, even his own Gardens, and threw up a number of extemporized shelters to accommodate the helpless multitude. The necessities of life were brought up from Ostia and the neighbouring municipalities, and the price of grain was

lowered to three sesterces. Yet his measures, popular as their character might be, failed of their effect; for the report had spread that, at the very moment when Rome was aflame, he had mounted his private stage, and, typifying the ills of the present by the calamities of the past, had sung the destruction of Troy.

Only on the sixth day, was the conflagration brought to an end at the foot of the Esquiline, by demolishing the buildings over a vast area and opposing to the unabated fury of the flames a clear tract of ground and an open horizon. But fear had not yet been laid aside, nor had hope yet returned to the people, when the fire resumed its ravages; in the less congested parts of the city . . . The second fire produced the greater scandal of the two, as it had broken out on the Aemilian property of Tigellinus and appearances suggested that Nero was seeking the glory of founding a new capital and endowing it with his own name. Rome, in fact, is divided into fourteen regions, of which four remained intact, while three were laid level with the ground: in the other seven nothing survived but a few dilapidated and half-burned relics of houses . . . There were those who noted that the first outbreak of the fire took place on the nineteenth of July, the anniversary of the capture and burning of Rome by the Senones . . .

However, Nero turned to account the ruins of his fatherland by building a palace, the marvels of which were to consist not so much in gems and gold, materials long familiar and vulgarized by luxury, as in fields and lakes and the air of solitude given by wooded ground alternating with clear tracts and open landscapes. The architects and engineers were Severus and Celer, who had the ingenuity and the courage to try the force of art even against the veto of nature and to fritter away the resources of a Caesar . . .

But neither human help, nor imperial munificence, nor all the modes of placating Heaven, could stifle scandal or dispel the belief that the fire had taken place by order. Therefore, to scotch the rumour, Nero substituted as culprits, and punished with the utmost refinements of cruelty, a class of men, loathed for their vices, whom the crowd styled Christians. Christus, the founder of the name, had undergone the death penalty in the reign of Tiberius, by sentence of the procurator Pontius Pilatus, and the pernicious superstition was checked for a moment, only to break out once more, not merely in Judaea, the home of the disease, but in the capital itself, where all things horrible or shameful in the world collect and find a vogue. First, then, the confessed members of the sect were arrested; next, on their disclosures, vast numbers were convicted, not so much on the count of arson as for hatred of the human race. And derision accompanied their end: they were covered with wild beasts' skins and torn to death by dogs; or they were fastened on crosses, and, when daylight failed were burned to serve as lamps by night. Nero had offered his Gardens for the spectacle, and gave an exhibition in his Circus, mixing with the crowd in the habit of a charioteer, or mounted on his car. Hence, in spite of a guilt which had earned the most exemplary punishment, there arose a sentiment of pity, due to the impression that they were being sacrificed not for the welfare of the state but to the ferocity of a single man.[7]

Thus is Tacitus' description. Only three of the fourteen districts of Rome were spared by the fire. Though Tacitus certainly mentions that, "when Rome was aflame, he [Nero] had mounted his private stage, and, typifying the ills of the present by the calamities of the past, had sung the destruction of Troy," it is Cassius Dio, writing more than a century later who is responsible for the story about Nero looking the part of lyre-player (fiddler) while Rome burned. Moreover, Tacitus has Nero in Antium at the time, whereas Dio places Nero at the palace in Rome. Note that Dio never says Nero "fiddled," but he does tell us that in the midst of the city burning, "While the whole population was in this state of mind and many, crazed by the disaster, were leaping into the very flames, Nero ascended to the roof of the palace, from which there was the best general view of the greater part of the conflagration, and assuming the lyre-player's garb, he sang the 'Capture of Troy,' as he styled the song himself, though to the enemies of the spectators it was the Capture of Rome."[8] From that statement, more than a hundred years after the fire, do we have the common impression of Nero playing the lyre while Rome burned. But of course, that is not exactly what Tacitus or even Dio says. Each claims Nero sang while Rome burned, which is not much better than playing the lyre, but an important distinction nonetheless.

Another significant piece of information from Tacitus' account is the way Nero developed the city following its hollowing out by the fire. As Tacitus tells us, Nero even considered renaming the city and "calling by his name" which would be something akin to, "Neropolis." With much of the city decimated, Nero went about building a palace for himself, known as the Domus Aurea, or the Golden House, whose remnants may still be seen today. The Imperial palace including the Domus Aurea extended from

---

7. Tacitus, *Annals*, 15.38–44.
8. Cassius Dio, *Roman History*, 62.18.1.

the Palatine Hill, where the Caesars from the time of Augustus lived, over to Monte Oppio. The valley between the two hills (Palatine and Oppian) was turned into a fish-pond, or rather a lake. Erected near the lake was a colossal statue of Nero himself as the sun-god. All of this was becoming too much for the populace, the Senate, and most of all the generals stationed in the borderlands, where talk of revolt was fomenting.

So Nero's delay in responding to the immediate crisis of the fire, and his subsequent attention to building projects, combined with his desire to rename Rome, "Neropolis" certainly fueled the rumors that he had the fire set deliberately. He needed a scapegoat. And as we read from Tacitus, Nero fastened the guilt on the Christians, "loathed for their vices" (Tacitus, *Annals*, 15.44).

Finally, it is noteworthy that Tacitus says arrests were first made of all those who pleaded guilty (to being Christian). Only a few years prior to the Great Fire, in 57 CE, Paul advised the Roman Christians to cooperate with the authorities.[9] Did these Christians simply follow Paul's advice, and his maxim that rulers are not a terror to good conduct but to bad? Did they simply admit to being Christian and hand over the names of others without knowing or expecting a violent end? At any rate, as Tacitus tells us, those who were arrested first then incriminated others. Then, Nero executed these Christians who "had earned the most exemplary punishment." It is during this persecution, the first of Roman authorities against Christians, that Peter and Paul are considered to have been martyred. Although, as we have seen, there is no direct evidence supporting this claim; it is only circumstantial.

The Jewish Revolt

Back in Jerusalem the people had been reeling under Roman rule. Caligula's desire to set up a statue of himself in the Jerusalem Temple, the Roman soldier exposing himself not long afterwards, and many other

---

9. "Let every person be subordinate to the higher authorities, for there is no authority except from God, and those that exist have been established by God. Therefore, whoever resists authority opposes what God has appointed, and those who oppose it will bring judgment upon themselves. For rulers are not a cause of fear to good conduct, but to evil. Do you wish to have no fear of authority? Then do what is good and you will receive approval from it, for it is a servant of God for your good. But if you do evil, be afraid, for it does not bear the sword without purpose; it is the servant of God to inflict wrath on the evildoer" (Rom 13:1–4).

innumerable slights and deliberate provocations that inevitably happen with an occupying force grew to be too much for the people. They wanted to live according to their own religious law (Mosaic Law) and be a free, self-determining people.

In addition, James known as the "brother of the Lord," a.k.a. "James the Just," was a living witness to Jesus and the apparent leader in Jerusalem of the movement started by Jesus. We are told that James drank no wine, ate no meat, and prayed so often that his knees resembled those of a camel's. After the Roman procurator Festus died suddenly in 62 CE, and before his replacement arrived, the high priest Ananus arrested James (the brother of Jesus, a.k.a, "the brother of the Lord" in the New Testament) and had him executed on the charges of violating Mosaic Law (Josephus, *Antiquities*. 20.9.1). This so enflamed the resident population that Ananus had to give up the high priesthood before the new Roman governor arrived. The martyrdom of James the Just was thought by some Jews and later Christians to be the theological reason for the Jerusalem siege (Eusebius, *EH* 2.23.19). Such was the situation in Jerusalem in the early 60s.

Shortly after the great fire of Rome, but in no way related, the simmering tensions between Jews and their Roman occupiers in Judea boiled over in 66 CE. Jews in Judea protested the taxation polices of the Romans. In want of cash, the Romans raided the Temple treasury which infuriated the Jews and led to open revolt, driving out the pro-Roman King Herod Agrippa II, and his sister Berenice. These are the same two who, a few years earlier, with the Roman governor Festus, had heard Paul's appeal to Caesar (see Acts 25:13—26:30). Now the Roman governor of Syria sent an entire legion (about 5000 soldiers) to crush the rebellion, but it was defeated by the Jewish rebels. This devastating loss roused slumbering Rome. Nero placed the cool-headed Vespasian as first in command with orders to defeat the insurgency. Vespasian's son Titus was his second. And Vespasian's second son, Domitian, was there to lend support.

By the time Vespasian and his armies arrived in Judea in 67 CE, Jerusalem was a fortress, though plagued by internal rivalries. Rather than a direct assault, Vespasian led his forces and those of Agrippa II through Galilee crushing weaker defenses. At one point, a captured commander of Galilean forces by the name of Josephus was brought before Vespasian. Josephus claimed that Jewish prophecies indicated that Vespasian would be ruler of the world. Vespasian dismissed such stories and had Josephus taken away as a prisoner of war (Josephus, *The Jewish War*, 3.8.9). Titus participated in the war effort and in his spare time began an affair with Berenice, who was eleven years younger than him.

Meanwhile in Rome, things were not going well for Nero. His maniacal ways had spurned open talk of rebellion by at least two generals. The populace was even mocking Nero by hanging insulting signs around the city and spreading rumors of his impending demise. Finally driven nearly mad, he fled the city and committed suicide on June 9, 68. He was thirty years old. By this time Vespasian's forces had wiped out nearly all significant opposition and were ready to begin a siege of Jerusalem. But after Nero committed suicide, all military actions on the part of Vespasian ceased, as he awaited orders from the new emperor.

The Year of the Four Emperors

Shortly after Nero's death there was a quick succession of those vying for the purple. General Galba, one of those generals who had been in open revolt against Nero, assumed control. Agrippa II and Titus set sail for Rome to meet with Galba. They made it as far as Greece when Galba was assassinated on January 15, 69. At this point Titus returned to Caesarea in Judea and Agrippa continued on to Rome.

Galba had been assassinated by forces from General Otho, a friend of the departed Nero. In fact, at one point Nero had carried on an affair with Otho's wife, Poppaea Sabina, who left Otho and married Nero. This is the same Poppaea whom Nero kicked to death while she was pregnant. For his part, Otho reigned only three months before he committed suicide when it was clear that forces led by General Vitellius were intent on overthrowing him and making Vitellius emperor. Thus, Vitellius assumed the throne on April 16, 69.

In the meantime, Jerusalem was still a city divided by two factions. One, the sicarii, led by Simon bar Giora (son of Gioras), whose primary headquarters was Masada, and the other, the zealots, led by John, son of Levi, of Giscala, who used the Temple as their headquarters. As Josephus tells it, "those who ran away from John had a more murderous reception from Simon, and anyone who eluded the tyrant within the walls was killed by the tyrant outside the gates. Thus for those who wished to desert to the Romans every way of escape was cut off."[10] So at this point the Romans

---

10. Josephus, *The Jewish War*, 4.558, in Williamson, *Josephus: The Jewish War*, 279.

simply surrounded the city and let the warring factions in and around Jerusalem have at it.

By this time, Vespasian's own men and Berenice herself were pressing him into service, telling him that he would be a better emperor than any other. Vespasian also recalled the captured Galilean commander who had prophesied that Vespasian would be ruler of the world, and had him released. From that point on, the elated and vindicated Josephus became a mouthpiece for the Romans, eventually negotiating with the city of Jerusalem for its surrender. Vespasian became convinced that he would be emperor and in turn sent forward troops to Rome while he secured the grain supply and support of the province of Egypt. In this Vespasian was accompanied by Agrippa II among others. In Egypt, soon stories began circulating of Vespasian healing the blind! (Cassius Dio 66). Before Vitellius could acquiesce, for he knew his own support was dwindling, Vespasian's soldiers assassinated him on Dec 22, 69. Thus concluded the "year of the four emperors," with Vespasian in clear command. Though he was still in Alexandria, Egypt, his power in Rome and throughout the empire was now consolidated.[11]

Destruction of the Jerusalem Temple

With Vespasian now firmly in command of the empire, his son Titus could focus on wrapping up operations in Judea, which were by now squarely focused on the siege of Jerusalem. Josephus acted on behalf of the Romans and spoke to the factions in Jerusalem in a vain attempt to secure their surrender. Instead, Josephus became a witness to the destruction of the Temple and much of the city. He later wrote a first-person account of these events called, *The Jewish War*.

But in 70 CE the siege of Jerusalem was brutal. Josephus describes a truly pitiable site with one mother resorting to cannibalizing her infant children to stay alive. The Temple and most of the city was razed to the ground that year, after which Titus returned to Rome without Berenice where a grand triumph was celebrated in honor of Vespasian, Titus, and Domitian. The remaining vestiges of Judean opposition were snuffed out at Masada in 74 CE. (Josephus' depiction of the triumph is reproduced in the section on the Arch of Titus below.)

---

11. For more on this fascinating year in Roman history, see Morgan, *69 A.D.*

The Flavians (69–96)

Vespasian and his wife Flavia Domitilla the Elder had three children: Flavia Domitilla the younger, Titus (r. 79–81 CE), and Domitian (r. 81–96 CE). After Vespasian returned to Rome to claim the imperial title, he reigned ten years, until 79 CE. Titus reigned briefly, succumbing to an acute illness shortly after he came to power. Domitian's reign was a much longer fifteen years. Thus the Flavian dynasty lasted nearly thirty years, from 69–96.

Flavia Domitilla the younger had a daughter named simply Flavia Domitilla, who in turn married a certain Titus Flavius Clemens who was the son of Sabinus III, and great nephew of Vespasian.[12] The married couple, Flavia Domitilla and Titus Flavius Clemens, had two sons who were renamed "Titus" and "Domitian" by the emperor Domitian and made his heirs. Titus Flavius Clemens even served as consul with Domitian in 95 CE. But something happened to turn Domitian against the couple for in a surprising twist, Titus Flavius Clemens was brought up on charges of atheism and condemned to death; whereas Flavia Domitilla was exiled. The charge of atheism was with respect to the Roman gods. It was a charge sometimes leveled against Jews who would not acknowledge or worship the Roman gods. We will explore this intriguing story in more depth when we see the Domitilla catacombs, named for Flavia Domitilla.

Titus might be considered the favored son. He was second in command to his father in the Jewish War. He was given command of the military operation when Vespasian went to Rome to claim the purple. Around 75 CE both Agrippa II and Berenice moved to Rome. Berenice lived with Titus and they might have been married if it were not for political opposition. She ultimately left Rome at Titus' bequest (Dio Cassius 65.15). Titus also oversaw the opening games at the Colosseum and celebrated his victory over the Jewish people with a commemorative arch in close proximity to the amphitheater. Perhaps unfortunately, he had a short reign (79–81 CE) after his father's death.

Domitian, as the second son of Vespasian, seemed to suffer by comparison with Titus. Domitian's reign was punctuated by a cruelty not seen since the time of Nero, even though Domitian reigned longer than any emperor since Tiberius. As a sign of his arrogance, Domitian referred to himself in the first person royal plural as "Our Lord and God," which became the title he used in both writing and conversation (Suetonius, *Domitian*,

---

12. Sabinus III was the son of Flavius Sabinus, who was the older brother of Vespasian.

13.2, in *Lives of the Caesars*). Interestingly it was during Domitian's reign that the Gospel of John was likely composed, with Thomas' claim that Jesus is "My Lord and God" (John 20:28). In the end, Domitian was assassinated by court officials (including Stephanus, Domitilla's steward!) and he was succeeded by his advisor Nerva, thus ending the Flavian dynasty.

Colosseum and the Arch of Titus

Among the many accomplishments of the Flavian dynasty is the longest lasting (literally): the Flavian Amphitheater, better known as the Colosseum. Upon returning to Rome from the Jewish war, Vespasian was incredulous to learn the Nero had built a lake in the middle of the city for his own personal use. In a stroke of political genius, Vespasian returned the land and the lake to the people for their use. The lake was drained and in its place was constructed a fantastic amphitheater, inaugurated in 80 CE, ten short years after construction began. The amphitheater was situated near the colossal statue of Nero, thus the amphitheater's nickname, the Colosseum. But an amphitheater was not enough for the Flavians. In addition, to commemorate Titus' victory over the God of Carmel (Yahweh) and the Jewish people, Titus erected an arch near the Flavian Amphitheater. Thus these two architectural masterpieces conceived of and constructed by the Flavians, have become symbols of Roman power, domination, and might.

Curtain Closes on the First Century

With Nerva succeeding the assassinated Domitian, the Flavian Dynasty came to an end. Nerva, though elected by the Senate, had a short fifteen-month reign (96–98 CE). Still, he had the foresight (and the compulsion) to choose an heir, thus saving the empire from the throes of civil war. Perhaps his greatest achievement was a peaceful transition after his death, for the succeeding emperors presided over a relatively peaceful time, as their lengthy reigns indicate: Trajan 98–117; Hadrian 117–138; Antoninus 138–161; and Marcus Aurelius 161–180. Far from the year of 69 which saw four emperors, the four emperors who followed Nerva reigned a combined eighty-two years.

The tumult, chaos, civil war, destruction, fire, and persecution of the first century was the soil in which Christianity grew in the capital of the Empire. The second and third centuries saw more stability and growth with sporadic, localized outbreaks of persecution. By the end of the first quarter of the fourth century Christianity was a "licit religion," and shortly thereafter was the official religion of the empire. Our understanding of this religion's beginnings in the capital of the empire will give us more appreciation for its enduring hold on the human imagination, as well as lessons that may be applicable today.

Part II

3

The Vatican Area

THE CITY OF ROME is inextricably associated with the Apostle Peter in our collective Christian imagination. The iconic power of St. Peter's Basilica demonstrates the eventual victory of Christian Rome over pagan Rome. In a contest, the Petrine Basilica would also edge out the Pauline when it comes to Roman renown. Show someone an image of the dome of Saint Peter's Basilica and you can be sure that the person will identify the city of Rome. Show someone the Basilica of St. Paul Outside the Walls, and fewer people will make the connection to Rome. Over the millennia, the hearts of devoted pilgrims have combined with the ambitious plans of popes and the curia to link indelibly the city of Rome with St. Peter, establishing their combined primacy and centrality in the Catholic faith and the Christian imagination.

THE ROME OF PETER AND PAUL—PART II

The Vatican before Peter

It is helpful to understand something of the pre-Christian history of the area which is now St. Peter's Basilica. In antiquity, the Ager Vaticanus, (area of land on the other side of the Tiber, around Mons Vaticanus) was outside the city of Rome proper. The area was known for its clay-fired dishes and poor quality wine: "Drink Vatican [wine] if you like vinegar" or "you drink Vatican. You drink poison."[1] There were small family estates here, used by the wealthy to escape the crowded city. By the time of Augustus, the region of the Vatican became the fourteenth district of the city, though it was still considered in some respects outlying area. Not long afterwards, to accommodate a growing population with its thirst for games and entertainment, the Vatican also became the site of a park known as the Horti Agrippinae, or the gardens of Agrippina (the elder). These gardens were near the Tiber, laid out by Germanicus for his wife Agrippina, and were passed on to her son, Gaius who became Emperor Caligula. Eventually, the gardens passed to Nero. But the Vatican was also the site of a circus and structures for entertainment including the naumachiae (where mock sea battles were staged). Along the two roads that crossed the area, the Via Cornelia[2] and the Via Triumphalis were cemeteries, attesting to the fact that this land was earlier outside the city of Rome (as it was illegal and improper to bury the dead within the city limits). (See the maps on pages 22 and 49).[3]

Interestingly, there was a temple in the Ager Vaticanus (Vatican field) known as the Phrygianum or the shrine of Cybele, the Magna Mater (great mother). She was attended by eunuch priests and her cult (and image) was brought from Phrygia (central Asia minor, the Kingdom of Pergamum) to Rome during the second Punic war (218–201 BCE). The Romans were following the advice of an oracle that said Carthage could be defeated if Rome imported Cybele. The main temple to Cybele was on the Palatine, but the Ager Vaticanus was the site of another. This Vatican temple remained until at least the fourth century, where the cult of Cybele continued alongside

---

1. Martial, *Epigrams* 10.45.5 and 6.92.3. See also 12.48.14, "the treacherous, flat content of a Vatican jar," and Cicero, "Our Vatican and Pupinian fields will certainly appear not fit to be compared with [the Campanians'] rich and fertile plains" (*On the Agrarian Law* 2.35.96 in Cicero, *Pro Quinctio*).

2. In the Middle Ages two prominent tombs stood near the place where the Via Cornelia linked the Pons Aelius and the Mausoleum of Hadrian: Meta Romuli and the Terebinthus.

3. For more information on this see Toynbee and Ward-Perkins, *The Shrine of St. Peter*, 3–23.

the Basilica of St. Peter. Archeological remains of this temple were found in the Piazza San Pietro. The image below shows the ancient Via Cornelia, the Vatican hill, and the Circus of Gaius.[4]

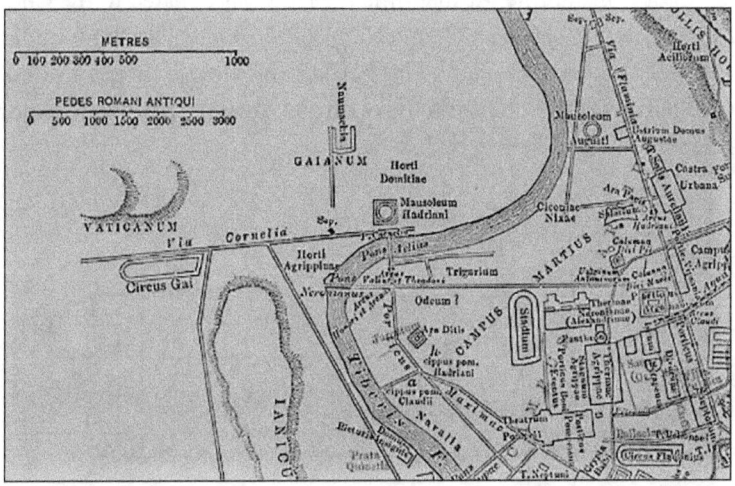

Peter's Tomb

Guides at St. Peter's will tell us with great conviction that it was during Nero's persecution of the Christians, following the great fire of 64, that Peter and Paul were martyred. Peter would have been taken out of the city, across the Tiber to the Vatican Circus (the gardens of Agrippina, by that time the gardens of Nero), and executed as a non-citizen in a typical Roman way for the time, by crucifixion. Peter insisted he was unworthy to die in a manner like that of his Lord. So the soldiers crucified him upside down (*Acts of Peter* 37). One of the last images Peter would have seen would have been the 98-foot-tall, 331-ton obelisk that now stands in the piazza.[5]

    4. Platner, *Topography*. Image in Public Domain. Digital image from https://upload.wikimedia.org/wikipedia/commons/0/02/The_Topography_and_Monuments_of_Ancient_Rome_QNO.jpg.

    5. Pliny speaks of the obelisk in his *Natural History* when he says, "the third obelisk in Rome stands in the Vatican Circus [in Vaticano ... circo] that was built by the emperors Gaius and Nero. It was the only one of the three that was broken during its removal. It was made by Nencoreus, the son of Sesosis; and there still exists another that belongs to him: it is 100 cubits in height and was dedicated by him to the Sun-god in accordance with an oracle after he had been stricken with blindness and had then regained his sight" (Pliny, *Natural History*, 36.74). There is debate about whether the obelisk that stands

Peter would have been buried in a pauper's grave behind the circus, in the vicinity of a first-century cemetery. There is archeological evidence to indicate that a small shrine commemorating the location existed here, until the reign of Constantine. At that time the land was donated to the Church, and the cemetery was partially buried in order to create a flat foundation for the first basilica of St. Peter. This basilica was erected in 324 around the reputed burial site of Peter, with the main altar over the previous memorial, represented by the diagram by Lanciani.[6]

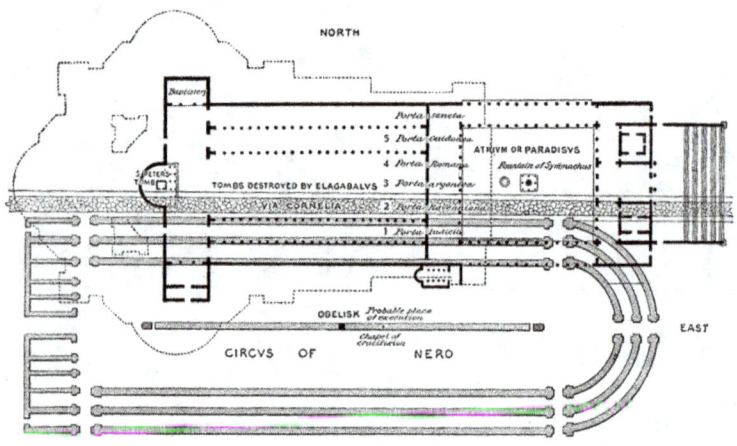

today in the piazza is one or the other of the obelisks Pliny mentions. Most likely it is the "third" obelisk, though we have to understand "in circo" as meaning "in the vicinity of the circus" rather than literally in the circus, as archaeological data now confirms that the original location of the piazza obelisk was near a cemetery, and not at the center of the circus as Lanciani would have it (above). Modern Vatican scholars make a case for the obelisk originally standing in Heliopolis, Egypt, and associating Nencoreus with Pharaoh Amenemhet II (1985–1929 BCE). In 40 CE Cornelius Gallus, the Roman prefect of Egypt, reduced its height and moved it to the Forum of Julius in Alexandria, Egypt. The Emperor Gaius (Caligula) had it moved to his circus in Rome (which later became the circus of Nero). Not until the renovation of Saint Peter's Basilica was the obelisk moved to its present site. Papi, *San Pietro in Vaticano*, 29. (The Church reused the basic materials, architectural forms, hierarchical organizations, poetry, music and language of the classical world following the tradition of Augustine, who advised in *On Christian Doctrine* that Christians utilize the intellectual goods of the classical world in accord with the scriptural example of the Israelites who fled Egypt with the plunder of gold and silver.)

6. Diagram from Lanciani, *Pagan and Christian Rome*, 128. Image in public domain. Digital image from: http://penelope.uchicago.edu/Thayer/E/Gazetteer/Places/Europe/Italy/Lazio/Roma/Rome/Vatican/S.Peter/Lanciani_plan.html.

And the following seventeenth-century diagram illustrates something similar.⁷

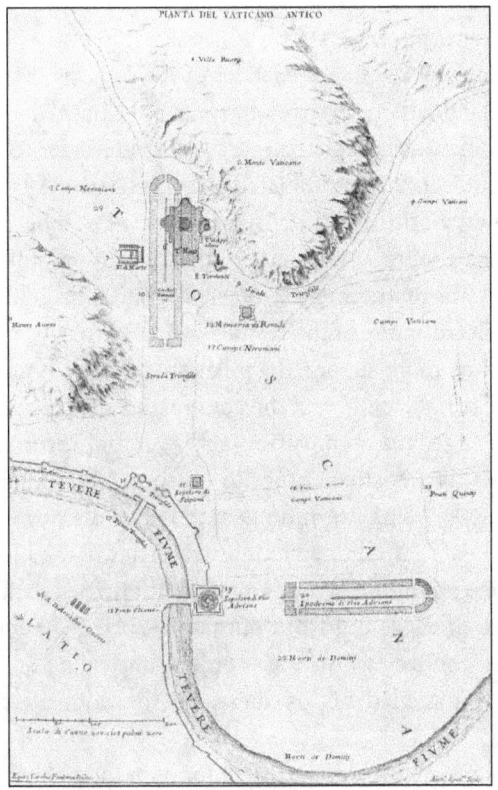

The Renovation

This basilica stood for over a millennium, until it was "renovated." Pope Nicholas V in 1452 made plans to repair the crumbling edifice which was in danger of collapse in certain sections. Not until 1506 did Pope Julius II lay the first stone of an extraordinarily ambitious project which would not merely repair the old Church but replace it with something even more glorious. Three years earlier Julius had named Bramante chief architect of the project. Though Bramante was a gifted architect (he built the

---

7. Fontana, *Templum Vaticanum*. Image in public domain. Digital image from http://www.roger-pearse.com/weblog/wp-content/uploads/2014/05/fontana_1_plan_of_ancent_vatican.jpg.

Tempietto at San Pietro in Montorio in 1502), he earned the nickname, *Bramante ruinante* (Bramante the destroyer), because after his demolition of the basilica was nearly complete, he died! He did not live to realize his vision of a renovation.

In 1514 Raphael became the leader of the project and he was eventually succeeded by the then seventy-one-year-old Michelangelo (d. 1564) in 1547, whose dome was completed in 1593. Carlo Maderno was appointed chief architect in 1603. He completed the nave and the façade, the latter in 1614. The new basilica was consecrated on November 18, 1626, proclaimed to be the 1300th anniversary of the dedication of the first basilica. In 1629 Bernini was made chief architect, a position he held for nearly fifty years. He completed many of the statues inside the basilica, including that of Longinus, in the main supporting pillar to the right of the papal altar, as well as the bronze baldachin, and the colonnade outside.

The nearly 150-year renovation and eventual reconstruction of St. Peter's Basilica was a costly venture to be sure. Not coincidentally, at this point in history the selling of indulgences reached a peak. In fact, sponsored by Pope Leo X (Medici), a Dominican friar named Johannes Tetzel (1465–1519), led an indulgence campaign with jingles such as: "when the coin in the box rings, a soul from purgatory springs." Such crass appeal to cash aroused the ire of a young monk by the name of Martin Luther (1483–1546), who nailed his 95 theses to the door at the Wittenberg Castle church.

Theses 50, 51, and 86 are pertinent for our study here:[8]

- 50. Christians are to be taught that if the pope knew the exactions of the pardon-preachers, he would rather that St. Peter's church should go to ashes, than that it should be built up with the skin, flesh and bones of his sheep.

- 51. Christians are to be taught that it would be the pope's wish, as it is his duty, to give of his own money to very many of those from whom certain hawkers of pardons cajole money, even though the church of St. Peter might have to be sold.

- 86. Again: — Why does not the pope, whose wealth is to-day greater than the riches of the richest, build just this one church of St. Peter with his own money, rather than with the money of poor believers?

8. Martin Luther, "Disputation of Doctor Martin Luther on the Power and Efficacy of Indulgences," in *Works of Martin Luther*, 34, 37.

As the Reformation took hold, the Church in Rome found itself on the defensive in Europe, where much Rome's power and influence was lost within a period of 25 years. By the time the Council of Trent began in 1545, the Church in union with the bishop of Rome was a shadow of what she had been. So, in the midst of the Counter-Reformation, the construction of St. Peter's became a symbol of the efforts of the Church to reaffirm her authority and power.

Despite some objections to its funding, the popes continued building the monument and employed some of the greatest architects and artists of the day, including some we have mentioned, Bramante, Raphael, Michelangelo, Bernini, and many others. Built in the midst of the Reformation, in many respects the basilica incorporated a triumphalist tone that displays the church victorious. The monument recognizes not only St. Peter, but the power of the successor of Peter. It would not be unfair to recognize it as a sort of "imperial propaganda." Yet it was also for the honor and glory of God. The popes hired the best architects and artists not only because they could, but because the project was worthy of the Church's resources. St. Peter's Basilica was not going to be built "on the cheap."

As the Reformation and the reconstruction and building of St. Peter's happened simultaneously, we may consider here some of the church teaching about salvation that no doubt provided a backdrop to the vitriolic debates between Catholics and Protestants.

- There is but one universal church of the faithful, outside of which no one at all can be saved (Fourth Lateran Council, 1215).

- We declare, say, define, and pronounce that it is absolutely necessary for the salvation of every human creature to be subject to the Roman Pontiff (Pope Boniface VIII, Papal Bull *Unam Sanctam*, 1302).

- The most Holy Roman Church firmly believes, professes and preaches that none of those existing outside the Catholic Church, not only pagans, but also Jews and heretics and schismatics, can have a share in life eternal; but that they will go into the eternal fire which was prepared for the devil and his angels, unless before death they are joined with Her; and that so important is the unity of this ecclesiastical body that only those remaining within this unity can profit by the sacraments of the Church unto salvation, and they alone can receive an eternal recompense for their fasts, their almsgiving, their other works of Christian piety and the duties of a Christian soldier. No one, even if he pour out his blood for the Name of Christ, can be saved, unless he remain within the bosom and the unity of the Catholic Church (Pope Eugenius IV, Papal Bull, Cantate Domino, 1441).

When examining the style and symbolism of the current basilica, one can recognize the strong triumphal Roman vision of the Church throughout.

Entering St. Peter's

If one visits the basilica at dawn, the setting will be serene. It is "quiet hours," when no talking is allowed. We will usher past the statues of great saints and walk beneath the words of Jesus to Peter, "You are rock, and on this rock I will build my church" (Matth 16:20). The basilica is not only in honor of Peter, but also in honor of Roman Catholicism, and even in honor of the Pope who oversaw part of the final phase of the construction, Paul V (r. 1605–1621). (Note his name, central on the façade: Paulus V Burghesius Romanus.)[9]

As we approach St. Peter's we see the 132.5-meter-high dome, designed by Michelangelo, though he did not live to see its completion. The statues of Peter and Paul flank each side of the courtyard. As we enter the atrium we might be so eager to go into the basilica that we miss a few important details. In the ceiling are stuccoes depicting the life of Peter from his introduction to Jesus including his denial of Jesus and subsequent rehabilitation, to the stories about him in Acts of the Apostles, and apocryphal stories such as Domine, quo vadis. In one stucco, based on the *Golden Legend*, Peter and Paul appear to Constantine in a dream to assist him in being healed of leprosy.[10] The final stucco in the series depicts the construction of the basilica of St. Peter. Thus, the life of Peter from his call to the construction of the basilica that bears his name, is depicted in the ceiling stuccoes done by Carlo Maderno in the early seventeenth century, and there are three in honor of Pope Paul V himself.

---

9. The full Latin text on the façade is this: IN HONOREM PRINCIPIS APOST. PAVLVS V BVRGHESIVS ROMANVS PONT. MAX. AN. MDCXII PONT. VII (translated: in honor of the Prince of the Apostles, Paul V Borghese, Roman, Pontiff, in the year 1612, the seventh of his pontificate, [made this]).

10. De Voragine and Ryan, *Golden Legend*, 64.

THE VATICAN AREA

A. Coat of Arms of Pope Paul V
1. Andrew presents Peter to Jesus (John 1:40–41)
2. Calling of Peter and Andrew (Matt 4:18–22)
3. Miraculous catch of fish (Luke 5:1–11; John 21:1–11)
4. Jesus walking on the water to rescue Peter (Matt 14:22–33)
5. Handing over the keys (Matt 16:16–20)
6. Transfiguration (Matt 17:1–16)
7. Coin in the fish's mouth (Matt 17:24–27)
8. Jesus washes Peter's feet at Last Supper (John 13:1–11)
9. Jesus finds Peter, James, and John sleeping in the Garden of Gethsemane (Matt 26:40)
10. Peter cuts off ear of Malchus (John 18:10)
11. Peter denies Jesus before the maid (Matt 26:69–70)
12. Jesus sees Peter deny him a third time (Luke 22:60–62)
13. Peter and the Beloved Disciple at the tomb (John 20:1–10)
14. Peter recognizes Jesus at Lake Tiberias (John 21:7)
15. Feed my sheep (John 21:15–17)
16. Peter heals man crippled from birth (Acts 3:1–10)
17. Death of Ananias (Acts 5:1–6)
18. Death of Sapphira (Acts 5:7–11)
19. Peter raises Tabitha from the dead (Acts 9:36–43)
20. Peter's vision of the unclean animals (Acts 10:9–16)
21. Peter meets Cornelius the Gentile (Acts 10:25)
22. Peter rescued from prison by an angel (Acts 12:1–8)
23. Peter led away from prison by an angel (Acts 12:9–10)
24. Peter causes Simon Magus to fall (Acts of Peter)
25. Peter baptizes Processus and Martinianus (Acts of Peter)

26. Domine, quo vadis? (Acts of Peter)
27. The crucifixion of Peter (Acts of Peter)
28. The burial of Peter (Acts of Peter)
29. Greek Christians hide bodies of Peter and Paul in a well (Letter from Gregory to Constantina)[11]
30. Cornelius (Pope, 251–53 CE) and Lucina remove bodies of Peter and Paul from the well (*Liber Pontificalis*)[12]
31. Peter and Paul appear to Constantine in a dream (*Golden Legend*)
32. Constantine begins construction of the Basilica of St. Peter

With our eyes still on the ceiling we are drawn to a stunning mosaic of the "Navicella," depicting Peter on the water with Christ, the same scene depicted in the ceiling above in stucco 4 according to our numbering. The mosaic is for the most part a seventeenth-century reproduction of the original, which dates from the early fourteenth century. New Testament students and others will immediately recognize the scene from Matthew 14:22–32.

> Then he made the disciples get into the boat and precede him to the other side, while he dismissed the crowds. After doing so, he went up on the mountain by himself to pray. When it was evening he was there alone. Meanwhile the boat, already a few miles

---

11. In a letter from Gregory the Great to Constantina (Book 4 Letter 30), he mentions the legend of Greek Christians who attempted to take Peter and Paul's corpses to the East. But this letter does not mention a well. "But what shall I say about the bodies of the blessed apostles, when it is certain that at the time of their martyrdom, believers came from the East to recover their bodies, as if they were their own citizens? The bodies were taken as far as the second milestone of Rome, and were deposited in a place that is called the Catacombs. [Today known as the catacombs of San Sebastiano]. But when their whole multitude came together and tried to remove them from there, the violence of the thunder and lightning so terrified them and put them to flight through excessive fear, that they did not presume on any account to try such a thing again. But then the Romans went out there and raised the bodies of those who deserved it, by their piety towards the Lord, and put them in the places where they are now buried" (Martyn, *The Letters of Gregory the Great*, 311).

12. Though *LP* relates this story, its version does not include the reference to the well. The significant paragraph is reproduced here: "In his time, at the request of a certain lady Lucina, he took up the bodies of the apostles Saints Peter and Paul from the catacombs at night; in fact first of all the blessed Lucina took the body of St Paul and put it on her estate on the Via Ostiensis close to the place where he was beheaded; the blessed bishop Cornelius took the body of St Peter and put it close to the place where he was crucified, among the bodies of the holy bishops at the temple of Apollo on the Mons Aureus, on the Vatican at Nero's palace, on 29 June" (Davis, *Book of Pontiffs*, 9).

offshore, was being tossed about by the waves, for the wind was against it. During the fourth watch of the night, he came toward them, walking on the sea. When the disciples saw him walking on the sea they were terrified. "It is a ghost," they said, and they cried out in fear. At once (Jesus) spoke to them, "Take courage, it is I; do not be afraid." Peter said to him in reply, "Lord, if it is you, command me to come to you on the water." He said, "Come." Peter got out of the boat and began to walk on the water toward Jesus. But when he saw how (strong) the wind was he became frightened; and, beginning to sink, he cried out, "Lord, save me!" Immediately Jesus stretched out his hand and caught him, and said to him, "O you of little faith, why did you doubt?" After they got into the boat, the wind died down. Those who were in the boat did him homage, saying, "Truly, you are the Son of God."

Though the Gospels of Mark and John tell the story of Jesus walking on the water,[13] no other evangelist has the story of Peter walking on the water. That is unique to Matthew.

On the other side of the atrium, in relief we see another story critical to our understanding of Peter: *Pasce oves meas*, or "feed my sheep." This story, referred to as the rehabilitation of Peter by some modern scholars, is from John 21:15–17. It is called the "rehabilitation" as it is read in juxtaposition to the threefold denial of Jesus by Peter. This "rehabilitation" with its threefold declaration of Peter's love for Jesus is unique to John's gospel.

> When they had finished breakfast, Jesus said to Simon Peter, "Simon, son of John, do you love me more than these?" He said to him, "Yes, Lord, you know that I love you." He said to him, "Feed my lambs." He then said to him a second time, "Simon, son of John, do you love me?" He said to him, "Yes, Lord, you know that I love you." He said to him, "Tend my sheep." He said to him the third time, "Simon, son of John, do you love me?" Peter was distressed that he had said to him a third time, "Do you love me?" and he said to him, "Lord, you know everything; you know that I love you." (Jesus) said to him, "Feed my sheep."

On the right-hand side of the atrium is an equestrian statue of Constantine (ca. 272–337); Bernini sculpted the horse. The statue depicts the moment Constantine saw the vision of the cross with the words, *in hoc signo vincis*, "in this sign you will conquer" (the story as told by Eusebius is reproduced in the section on the Arch of Constantine). He saw the vision

---

13. Mark 6:45–52; John 6:16–21.

prior to attacking Maxentius at the Milvian bridge, spanning the Tiber just a few miles north of the ancient city, in October of 312. Constantine won the battle and attributed the victory to the Christian God.[14] Thus, the vision opened Constantine to Christianity. Soon after the victory Constantine issued the Edict of Milan (313) which recognized Christianity as an acceptable/legitimate religion. Twelve years later he called the Council of Nicea.

On the left-hand side of the atrium is Charlemagne (ca. 742–814), emperor of the Holy Roman Empire. Charlemagne was crowned emperor in the basilica of St. Peter on Christmas eve in 800 by Pope St. Leo III. We will see the precise stone over which he was crowned when we enter the basilica. Together the statues of Constantine and Charlemagne remind us of the church's relationship with temporal power through the centuries.

Each entrance gate to the atrium leads directly to a door. All but one door (the center) were made in the twentieth century to replace the walnut doors that were there earlier. The new doors are bronze. The doors are named from left to right: Door of Death, Door of Good and Evil, the Filarete Door (named for its maker), the Door of the Sacraments, and finally the Holy Door which is open only during jubilees.

The Filarete Door is important for our study of Peter and Paul in Rome. The door is named for the sculptor (1400–1469), who fashioned the doors over a period of twelve years, finally completing them in 1445. Though his name was Antonio Averlino (as the door itself indicates), he was known by the nickname, Filarete. The door was made for the first basilica, as Filarete's dates indicate, and were reincorporated here. The left panel is devoted to Paul and the right to Peter. The bottom panel on each side depicts their respective martyrdoms. So the left hand bottom panel shows the legend of Paul's sentencing by Nero, Paul's being led out to Aquae Salviae, and his decapitation. We can also see something like an angel, but really Paul himself, appearing from a cloud and handing the scarf back to Plautilla. We recall this legend from the fourth–fifth-century Latin account, the "*Passio Sancti Pauli Apostoli*" (The Passion of Saint Paul the Apostle) discussed above (page 17). Before his execution, Plautilla, a follower of Paul, gave him her scarf with which he blindfolded his eyes. Immediately following the execution, the scarf could not be found; but Plautilla is later

---

14. Yet, note that on the Arch of Constantine the victory is attributed not to Jesus or to the Christian God specifically, but to the inspiration of a divinity (and) the greatness of his (Constantine's) mind, INSTINCTV DIVINITATIS MENTIS MAGNITVDINE.

said to have the blood-stained scarf.[15] Or, as Filarete would have it, Plautilla was given (or she found?) the scarf with Paul's help.

On the right-hand bottom panel door we see depicted the crucifixion of Peter. In this panel too we see the pudgy Nero sentencing Peter to death. We can also see the metae, as a nod to these legendary tales about Peter being crucified, *inter duas metas*. In the fifteenth century, these legends were key to portraying the events in the lives and deaths of the apostles. On the left we see the Pyramid of Cestius which was known at the time as the Meta of Remus,[16] and on the right, the Meta of Romulus, which was near the Vatican. This is a clear indication that Filarete believed, as did his contemporaries, that St. was crucified not in the Ager Vaticanus, or even the Circus of Nero (present day St. Peter's square), but on the Janiculum, where Bramante would later construct his Tempietto. So perhaps it is the pinnacle of irony that the center door of St. Peter's indicates that St. Peter was crucified elsewhere.

Through the doors we come to the nave of the basilica. The scale of the basilica itself makes it difficult to fully grasp its size. The proportions are such that the mind's eye is fooled to a degree. Only when we see something familiar such as a human being walking at the other end of the basilica does the enormity of the architecture begin to register with us.

We see a porphyry disk in the floor. This was in the original basilica of St. Peter, situated near the high altar. It is over this stone that Charlemagne and many other emperors (a total of twenty-three from 800 to 1452) were crowned by the Popes. In the renovation, the porphyry stone was moved from before the high altar to the entrance of the basilica where it remains today.

If we look to the left we will see one of many side chapels in this magnificent basilica. In particular we see the "chapel of the baptismal font" with a font made of red porphyry from the late imperial period. On the left of this chapel there is an eighteenth-century mosaic depicting the baptism of Processus and Martinianus by Peter. We immediately call to mind this legendary tale (reproduced in the appendix) and consider how important it was for the faith lives of Christians through the centuries.

Immediately behind us now, on the right-hand side of the basilica, we see perhaps the most famous of all Michelangelo's statues, *The Pietà*, in the "Chapel of the Pietà." Michelangelo was twenty-three years old when

---

15. Tajra, *Martyrdom of St. Paul*, 142.
16. See footnote 42 on page 24.

he was commissioned for this work carved from a single block of Carrara marble in 1499. It was his first and only work to bear his signature (on the belt): *Michael Angelus Bonarotus Florent[inus] faciebat* (faciebat is Latin for "made [this]"). Artistically, the statue is a masterpiece and was recognized as such upon its completion. Mary is depicted in her youth, not as an older woman. Jesus is depicted as a physically perfect human being, virtually untouched by his sufferings. Besides the nail-marks, there is no indication of the torture and beatings he suffered. In that way, Michelangelo represents the perfection of the incarnation of God.

We return to the central nave and approach the altar. On the floor we see markings indicating the length of some of the other major churches and basilicas in Christendom. Some find these markings strange; others see them as authentically Italian. St. Peter's depicts graphically that all other churches in Christendom do not measure up (so to speak) to it, the largest church in Christendom at 186.3 meters. The next largest is the Basilica of St. Paul in London at 158.1m, and so the floor shows until we get to the point of St. Patrick's Cathedral in New York at 101.19m. At that point in St. Peter's we are nearly at the high altar, having walked past the chapel of the Blessed Sacrament on the right, often concealed by drapes. The chapel is a quiet place for praying pilgrims in the midst of this massive monument that can at times seem too touristy.

At this point before the high altar, to our right is the bronze statue of St. Peter, whose foot has been worn down by the countless pilgrims who have touched it through the centuries. Scholars differ over the question of the statue's provenance. Dates range from the fifth to the thirteenth century. Opinion today seems to prefer the thirteenth century, with the possibility of Arnolfo di Cambio (ca. 1245–1310) as the artist. We recall (page 20 above) that the *Catalogus Liberianus* claimed that Peter was the founder of the church at Rome and served for 25 years, one month, and nine days, and that he took up this episcopate after Jesus' ascension. Despite some problems with this claim, it clearly established the length of Peter's episcopacy, and a legend developed that said no pope would serve as long as Peter.

Pope Pius IX proved that legend wrong when he celebrated his twenty-fifth anniversary as pope in the year 1871. He lived to celebrate his thirtieth anniversary, and died a year after that to become the longest serving pope (besides Peter) in Christendom.[17] The Vatican clergy commemorated the

---

17. Pope Pius IX's successor Leo XIII also served as Pope for twenty-five years. Pope St. John Paul II served longer than twenty-six years.

twenty-fifth anniversary of Pius IX's pontificate with the mosaic and Latin inscription above the baldachin for the bronze statue of Peter. Translated, the Latin inscription reads, "To Pius IX, pontiff, who was the one to equal the years of Peter in the Roman pontificate, the Vatican clergy decorated this sacred chair on June 16, 1871."

We turn our attention to the central octagon to see the massive pillars supporting the dome. In each pillar is a statue of a saint: Helen with the holy cross, Longinus with the spear, Veronica with the veil, and Andrew with a cross. St. Peter's basilica had or still has the relics from these saints in its reliquary: pieces from the true cross brought to Rome from Judea by Helen; the spear used by the Roman centurion to pierce the side of Jesus, the veil with which Veronica wiped the face of Jesus on the via dolorosa; and the head of Andrew, (brother of Peter), who was crucified on an 'X' cross. Many of these stories, their historical authenticity dismissed today, come from the medieval *Golden Legend*, which had become most authoritative by the time St. Peter's was rebuilt.

The Latin inscriptions in the internal face of the pillars read:

Veronica pillar	Helen pillar
HINC UNA FIDES	MUNDO REFVLGET
From here one faith	Shines on the world
Longinus pillar	Andrew pillar
HINC SACERDOTII	VNITAS EXORITVR
From here (the unity) of priests	Unity (of priests) pours forth

So taken together it reads: "From here one faith shines on the world" and "From here the unity of priests pours forth."

The papal altar is built over the *confessio*,[18] and over the papal altar we see the baldachin by Bernini. Only the pope may celebrate mass at this altar. During the renovation of the basilica there was a question about what if any relics to deposit at the base of the altar. Pope Clement VIII (1592–1605) responded that there was no need as the altar had already been built over the tomb of St. Peter.

The impressive bronze baldachin utilized a tremendous amount of bronze. Bernini went to Pope Urban VIII (from the Barberini family, whose insignia was a bee) who authorized him to take the bronze from the inside ribs of the dome of the Pantheon. When even that was not enough, Urban gave him the remaining bronze. Thus the quip, *quod non fecerunt barbari, Barberini fecerunt*, "what the Barbarians did not do, the Barberinis did." As a way to compensate for its loss, Bernini added two bell towers to the

---

18. The *confessio* is so named not because it is a reconciliation chapel, but because the Latin term *confessio* expresses something similar to the Greek term *martyrion*. A martyr confesses his or her faith to the point of death. Thus, the *confessio* is the place where the martyr's remains are. Usually they are at the base of the altar. In this case we see the bronze urn holding the pallia (plural of pallium).

The pallium has an interesting history, though the words of Walter Lippman may certainly apply, "the facts far exceed our curiosity." Nevertheless, the pallium is made of white wool from two lambs. The lambs are raised by the Trappist monks from the Abbey of the Three Fountains (the legendary site of Paul's martyrdom). The pope blesses the lambs on January 21 (feast day of St. Agnes, the name means "lamb") at Saint Agnes Outside the Walls on the Via Nomentana (not the St. Agnes in Agony at the Piazza Navona). At that point two sediari pontifici (corps that used to carry the pope, but now still carry out other ritual functions) deliver the lambs to the Benedictine sisters at the Basilica of St. Cecilia. On the feast of Saints Peter and Paul (June 29), metropolitan archbishops are invested with the pallium. Upon the death of an archbishop with two pallia, the first is rolled up and placed under his head. The most recent is placed around his neck. Below the urn holding the pallia are the relics of St. Peter. We see that on the scavi tour.

Pantheon. The Romans nicknamed them "the ass's ears of Bernini," and they were removed in 1883. Still, one can see the bees on the columns of the baldachin indicating that the project was "financed" by a member of the Barberini family, Pope Urban VIII.

At the apse of St. Peter's we see the chair of St. Peter itself. By legend the chair is one that Peter used while in Rome. Bernini encased it in bronze and displayed it here. A figure of the Holy Spirit as a dove hovers over the chair, signifying the divine authority which accompanies the office.

The four statues are the four great doctors of the church: two from the East and two from the West. On the far left hand side moving right we see St. Ambrose, St. Anastasius, Saint John Chrysostom, and St. Augustine. Each of the four is linked to the chair (by bronze drapery) signifying that they are in communion with the chair of Rome. The chair itself is not supported by the saints. The chair is self-supporting. What does this say about the way the church viewed itself at the time vis-à-vis Protestantism?

Finally, Bernini noted that the Trinity is depicted in that the mosaic in the dome represents God the Father, the cross over the baldachin represents Christ, and the dove as we have seen represents the Holy Spirit.

Many people who visit St. Peter's ask about the Latin and Greek inscriptions written in mosaic in the frieze around the basilica. Many are quotes or allusions to scripture, magnifying the authority, power, and wisdom of Peter, thereby magnifying the authority, power, and wisdom of the successor(s) of Peter.

On the left-hand side of the nave:

> EGO ROGAVI PRO TE O PETRE VT NON DEFICIAT FIDES TVA ET TV ALIQVANDO CONVERSVS CONFIRMA FRATRES TVOS

I have prayed for you O Peter that your faith may not fail; and once you have repented, strengthen your brothers (Luke 22:32).

On the right-hand side of the nave:

> QVODCVMQVE LIGAVERIS SVPER TERRAM ERIT LIGATVM ET IN COELIS ET QVODCVMQVE SOLVERIS SVPER TERRAM ERIT SOLVTVM ET IN COELIS

Whatever you bind on earth shall be bound in heaven; and whatever you loose on earth shall be loosed in heaven (Matt 16:19b).

On the dome:

TV ES PETRVS ET SVPER HANC PETRAM AEDIFICABO EC-
CLESIAM MEAM ET TIBI DABO CLAVES REGNI CAELORUM

You are Peter, and upon this rock I will build my church. I will give you the keys to the kingdom of heaven (Matt 16:18a, 19a).

Right-hand transept:

O PETRE DIXISTI TV ES CHRISTVS FILIVS DEI VIVI AIT
IESVS BEATVS ES SIMON BAR IONA QVIA CARO ET SANG-
VIS NON REVELAVIT TIBI

O Peter, you said you are the Christ the son of the living God and Jesus said Blessed are you, Simon son of Jonah, for flesh and blood has not revealed (this) to you (Matt 16:16–17).

Left-hand transept:

DICIT TER TIBI PETRE IESVS DILIGIS ME CVI TER O ELECTE
RESPONDENS AIS O DOMINE TV OMNIA NOSTI TV SCIS
QVIA AMO TE

Jesus said to you three times, "Peter do you love me?" To whom three times you the chosen responded, "O Lord you know everything, you know that I love you" (cf. John 21:17).

Apse, left side in Latin, right side in Greek (shorter form):

O PASTOR ECCLESIAE TV OMNES CHRISTI PASCIS AGNOS
ET OVES

O Shepherd of the church you feed all the lambs and sheep of Christ

ΣΥ ΒΑΣΚΕΙΣ ΤΑ ΑΡΝΙΑ ΣΥ ΠΟΙΜΑΙΝΕΙΣ ΤΑ ΠΡΟΒΑΤΙΑ
ΧΡΙΣΤΟΥ

You feed the lambs, you shepherd the sheep of Christ

And thus we like most visitors to St. Peter's Basilica are in awe over the majesty of this impressive architecture. We recall the gospel stories of this Galilean fisherman and wonder what he would think of this basilica to commemorate him in the Imperial capital. Peter has been honored in this place for centuries. Some of the world's most gifted artists, architects, sculptors, and painters gave their best work to this church. And thousands of unnamed Christians from throughout the Holy Roman Empire gave the widow's mite in indulgences said to release their loved ones from the pains of purgatory. It is difficult to see this mighty structure and not think that it might be more a monument to man than God. On the façade we see the Borghese family and Paul V's name displayed prominently. But where is Jesus? Perhaps it is not too surprising that one young energetic priest, Martin Luther, found himself appalled at the church for draining the coffers of the poor to build this monument. In many ways the building of this church planted the seeds of the Reformation. When we see this basilica we are moved to contemplate many matters of faith, service, history, theology, culture, and the sacred itself.

4

Colosseum, Saint Clement and Environs

Mamertine Prison
(Carcere Mamertino)

R ECENTLY I RECEIVED A flyer designed to promote interest in a Christian pilgrimage to Rome. There was featured prominently on day four of the visit, a trip to the Maritime(!) prison. Some poor editor let that slip and I suppose the eager pilgrims wondered if this was a prison by the sea. What we visit today is commonly known as the Mamertine (not maritime) prison, so named in the Middle Ages, but in the first century of the Common Era it was known as the Tullianum.

The Tullianum was in some ways akin to how people today might think of Alcatraz, only worse. It was meant for hardened criminals, enemies of the state, and lowlifes. It held prisoners such as Jugurtha (ca. 160–104 BCE, King of Numidia), Vercingetorix (ca. 72–46 BCE, chief of the Arverni, a Gallic tribe defeated by Julius Caesar), Simon bar Giora (fl. 68–70 CE, a leader of the Jewish revolt against the Romans in Jerusalem), the Catiline conspirators (ca. 63 BCE), and perhaps Sejanus (20 BCE–31 CE, prefect of the praetorian guard who tried to seize power from Tiberius).

There were two levels to the prison: an upper and a lower. The lower level seems originally to have been a cistern, and today is reached by a staircase. In republican times it was this level in particular that was known at the Tullianum. The Latin word *tullus* means "spring," and in fact, one can still hear a spring flowing in the lower level.

The Roman historian Livy (ca. 64 BCE–17 CE) without using the term "Tullianum," but mentioning a prison that overlooks the Forum, relates that it was made by the fourth king of Rome, Ancus Marcius (640–16 BCE) to stem lawlessness in the growing city (I.33). The author and Latin linguist Varro (116–27 BCE) connects the name Tullianum with the sixth king of Rome, Servius Tullius who would have ruled 575–35 BCE (*On the Latin Language* 5.151). And finally, the Roman politician Sallust (86–35 BCE) says this about the Tullianum:

> In the prison, when you have gone up a little way toward the left, there is a place called the Tullianum, about twelve feet below the surface of the ground. It is enclosed on all sides by walls, and overhead is a vaulted ceiling formed by stone arches; but neglect, darkness, and stench give it a hideous and terrifying appearance.[1]

As Sallust seems to indicate, the lower level Tullianum was essentially a chamber into which prisoners were dropped to be starved to death. The Tullianum was connected to the Cloaca Maxima, Rome's main sewer, through which the dead bodies of prisoners would be expelled into the Tiber. So it seems Alcatraz would be preferred to the Mamertine; St. Peter did not have a choice.

The sixth-century legend, *The Passion of Saints Processus and Martinianus, Martyrs* (and reproduced here in the appendix), says that Peter and Paul were condemned to the Mamertine for about nine months following the death of Simon Magus. In an episode that seems to reflect Acts of the

---

1. Sallust, *The War with Catiline*, 55.3–4.

Apostles 16:23-24 where Paul and Silas baptized their jailer, Processus and Martinianus witnessed Peter and Paul's miracles performed in prison and asked to be baptized. Fifty-seven fellow prisoners then asked to be baptized along with Processus and Martinianus, after which Peter and Paul celebrated Eucharist. According to the same legend, St. Peter eventually escaped and ran away along the Via Appia, where he lost a bandage. This location became the site of a church, known as *titulus fasciolae* or "church of the bandage." (Today it is known as the church of Ss. Nereus and Achilleus, though that association too has its difficulties.)[2] At any rate, the narrative of the sixth-century legend of Peter losing the bandage while departing the city then dovetails into the "Lord, where are you going" story, though in this it is "Domine, quo pergis" rather than "Domine, quo vadis."[3] Jesus replied, "I am going to Rome, to be crucified again." At that Peter turned around and returned to Rome to face his death.[4] The place of that legendary encounter is marked by the church that bears the name, "Domine, quo vadis."

Of course, the sixth-century legend of the baptism of Processus and Martinianus, as the Domine quo vadis legend, is late and not historical. The names of soldiers Processus and Martinianus and the story of their martyrdom go back to the time of Diocletian. And there was a church dedicated to them in Rome by the end of the fourth century. But they were not associated with Peter and Paul even by Pope Gregory the Great in the late sixth century.[5] So this mixing of Processus and Martinianus with Peter and Paul was a late development, reflected in the "Passio" that bears their name, but not by the Pope of the same era. Still the legend gives us a sense of the early medieval Christian imagination.

Another legend associated with the site can be seen along the stairwell leading from the upper level to the lower level. Today visitors see an impression in the stone (now covered by an iron grate) that is said to have been made when a soldier pushed Peter's head into the wall. This too is perhaps an interesting story but has no basis in history.

On the frieze on the front, we see the Latin inscription dedicated to the consuls who constructed the façade.

---

2. Petersen, "The Identification of the Titulus Fasciolae," 153.

3. Cf. Tajra, *Martyrdom of St. Paul*, 100. Cf. Passio Sanctorum Processi et Martiniani Martyrum, in Mombrizio, *Sanctuarium seu Vitae Sanctorum*, 2.403-4.

4. "The Acts of Peter," in *NTA* 2:313-14.

5. Eastman, *Ancient Martyrdom Accounts*, 29.

C · VIBIVS · C · F · RVFINVS · M · COCCEIVS · NERVA · COS · EX · S · C

Gaius Vibius Rufinus son of Gaius, and Marcus Cocceius Nerva, Suffect Consuls[6]

The two suffect consuls, Gaius Vibius Rufinus and Marcus Cocceius Nerva, would have repaired the prison in 22 CE,[7] and therefore we can imagine that if Peter and Paul were imprisoned here they would have read this same inscription. Also interesting to note is that Marcus Cocceius Nerva was the grandfather of Emperor Nerva (r. 96–98 CE).[8]

Thus the Mamertime prison has become a repository of legend and tall tales about the two pillars of the church at Rome.

Santa Maria in Aracoeli

The Aracoeli (altar of heaven) is so named because of a legend in the *Mirabilia* whereby Augustus Caesar himself learned through the Tiburtine Sibyl of the coming of Christ.

> And while Octavian diligently listened to the Sibyl, heaven opened, and a great brightness shone on him, and he saw in heaven a virgin exceedingly fair standing on an altar holding a man-child in her arms. Octavian marveled greatly at this, and he heard a voice from heaven saying: "This is the Virgin who shall conceive the Savior of the World." And again he heard another voice from heaven saying, "This is the altar of the Son of God." The emperor straightway fell to the ground and worshipped the Christ that should come. He showed this vision to the senators and they likewise marveled exceedingly. The vision took place in the chamber of the Emperor Octavian where the Church of the Santa Maria in Capitolio is now and where the Friars Minor are. Therefore it is called Santa Maria in Aracoeli.[9]

Though the legend would have us believe the church is built over the chamber of Octavian, archaeologically it is known that the church is built over the site of the ancient Roman arx, or citadel. Rather than a fort, this

---

6. A suffect consul was one who filled in for a consul who died, or who otherwise was not able to fulfill the term.

7. Aicher, *Rome Alive*, cf., CIL 6.1539.

8. *OCD*, *s.v.* Cocceius Nerva, Marcus.

9. Gardiner, *Marvels of Rome*, 17–18 (2.1).

was an area for sentries to keep watch over the city, and from which to sound an alarm. Sentries here would communicate with sentries on the Janiculum by means of flags. The arx was also important as the last refuge during the Gallic siege of 390–87 BCE. In 344 BCE the Romans erected a temple here to Juno Moneta, as it was believed Juno "warned" (*moneta* is Latin for "warned") the city of the impending attack of the Gauls. The Juno Moneta temple also served as the mint. Thus we derive our English word, "money."

A Christian church has been known to exist on this site since the sixth century, being renovated and restored at various points, and being transferred from Benedictines to Franciscans in 1250 by Innocent IV. Its legendary association with Octavian and its proximity to the heart of the city is reflected even today as it is dedicated to the city council of Rome. In the picture above we see its proximity to the Campidoglio, which is based on the Latin word, Capitoline. This area is still the center of Roman municipal affairs.

As we approach the church, one is struck by the fact that the façade was never completed. As we enter the church, notice the 22 columns of various sizes, taken from ancient Roman sites. Note in particular the third column on the left, on which we can read the inscription, *a cubiculo Augustorum*, and hearkening back to the legend that the vision of the Virgin Mary to Octavian took place in one of his chambers. Look in the floor for the funeral monument of the humanist Flavio Biondo, one of the first archaeologists, and also author of the three volume work *Rome Restored* [1444–1448]. This is the same church, but referred to as the Temple of Jupiter, where Gibbon says that: "It was at Rome, on the 15th of October, 1764, as I sat musing amidst the ruins of the Capitol, while the barefooted friars were singing vespers in the Temple of Jupiter, that the idea of writing the decline and fall of the city first started to my mind."[10]

In the apse we see the Virgin Mary and Augustus seated with the saints and angels. In the center of the north transept we see a seventeenth-century shrine to St. Helen, mother of Constantine, also known as the Santa Cappella, made of eight columns. The relics of Helen are thought to be here. Beneath the shrine are the remains of a medieval altar which depicts the vision to Augustus referenced above. Only in this depiction, the sibyl has been replaced by the Virgin Mary.

---

10. Gibbon, *The Autobiography of Edward Gibbon*, 160.

At the end of this transept, on the right, we find the Cappella del Santissimo Bambino, a figure of the baby Jesus, carved from olive wood from Gethsemane in the sixteenth century. Unfortunately, this figure was stolen in 1994 and has been replaced with a copy. Nevertheless, the bambino is the object of intense reverence and religious fervor even today. During Christmas and Epiphany the bambino is paraded through the throngs of people. For the Christmas feast day, the bambino is taken from his chapel and placed in a baroque throne, before being paraded to the nativity scene during the Gloria. Children and mothers alike place petitions before it and earnestly seek the bambino's intercession. He is brought out again at Epiphany and paraded to the top of the Aracoeli from which point the city and its people are blessed.

Those fortunate enough to participate in either of these liturgies will experience something of the Roman, thoroughly Italian, pageant of common religiosity. During the liturgy and accompanying bambino parade we might think of high-minded theological concepts we study in graduate courses, those ideas that occupy the thoughts of the learned. Do any of these concepts influence the masses? Is there a disconnect between the academy and the pew? What are the people proclaiming by their actions? By their placing written petitions before an olive wood statue of the baby Jesus? By their placing this statue in a throne and parading it about? What do they believe? Does that belief conform to "authentic Christianity?" Some who witness this pagent find it more Roman (in the sense of ancient Rome) than Christian. How has Christianity been able to incorporate indigenous peoples and their religious customs? It is here we see that not only Christianity has influenced Rome, but Rome has influenced Christianity.

Arch of Titus

This arch commemorates the Roman victory over the Jewish people in battles that took place from 66–74 CE, what Josephus writes about in his *The Jewish War*. Romans often commemorated military victories with such an arch, which depicted scenes from the battle or the triumphal procession (as we have here) in relief. Architecturally the arch is a masterpiece of proportion. When Napoleon Bonaparte saw it from near the Arch of Septimius Severus on the other side of the forum, he ordered his own architects to measure it exactly. Thus it inspired the Arc de Triomphe on the Champs Élysées in Paris.

Not only is the Arch of Titus quite graceful with its nearly flawless Pentelic marble,[11] it is the earliest surviving of all Roman triumphal arches. There would have been a bronze chariot (a quadriga with four horses)

---

11. Penteli is a mountain near Athens used as a source of marble in antiquity (e.g., the Parthenon), and even today. Pentelic marble is known for its purity.

COLOSSEUM, SAINT CLEMENT AND ENVIRONS

atop the arch. One can look beyond the arch to the Capitoline hill to the nineteenth-century monument of Vittorio Emanuelle to see how triumphal arches might have appeared in their days of glory, complete with the quadriga. These arches functioned as memorials to the victories of generals and emperors, as well as to the triumphal procession itself.

As we learned in part I of this tourbook (pages 34–36) [x-ref], after Vespasian went to Rome to claim the throne in 69 CE, he left his son Titus in Jerusalem to complete the siege and mop-up operations there. Titus achieved victory only one short year later and returned to Rome as victor.

The historian Josephus tells the story like this:

> 3. Titus, now proceeding on his projected march to Egypt, traversed the desert with all possible dispatch and reached Alexandria. Here, having determined to sail for Italy, he dismissed to their respective former stations the two legions which had accompanied him, the fifth to Moesia, the fifteenth to Pannonia. Of the prisoners, the leaders, Simon and John, together with seven hundred of the rank and file, whom he had selected as remarkable for their stature and beauty, he ordered to be instantly conveyed to Italy, wishing to produce them at the triumph. After a voyage as favorable as he could have desired, Rome gave him such a reception and welcome as it had given to his father; but with the added luster that Titus was met and received by his father himself. The crowd of citizens was thus afforded an ecstasy of joy by the sight of the three princes now united. Before many days had elapsed they decided to celebrate their achievements by one triumph in common, though the senate had decreed a separate triumph to each. Previous notice having been given of the day on which the pageant of victory would take place, not a soul among that countless host in the city was left at home: all issued forth and occupied every position where it was but possible to stand, leaving only room for the necessary passage of those upon whom they were to gaze.
>
> 4. The military, while night still reigned, had all marched out in companies and divisions, under their commanders, and been drawn up, not round the doors of the upper palace, but near the temple of Isis; for there the emperors reposed that night. At the break of dawn, Vespasian and Titus issued forth, crowned with laurel and clad in the traditional purple robes, and proceeded to the Octavian walks; for here the senate and the chief magistrates and those of equestrian rank were awaiting their coming. A tribunal had been erected in front of the porticoes, with chairs of ivory placed for them upon it; to these they mounted and took

their seats. Instantly acclamations rose from the troops, all bearing ample testimony to their valor: the princes were unarmed, in silk robes and crowned with bays. Vespasian, having acknowledged their acclamations, which they wished to prolong, made the signal for silence; then amidst profound and universal stillness he rose and, covering most of his head with his mantle, recited the customary prayers, Titus also praying in like manner. After the prayers, Vespasian, having briefly addressed the assembled company, dismissed the soldiers to the customary breakfast provided for them by the emperors, and himself withdrew to the gate which, in consequence of the triumphal processions always passing through it has thence derived its name. Here the princes first partook of refreshment, and then, having donned their triumphal robes and sacrificed to the gods whose statues stood beside the gate, they sent the pageant on its way, driving off through the theatres, in order to give the crowds an easier view.

5. It is impossible adequately to describe the multitude of those spectacles and their magnificence under every conceivable aspect, whether in works of art or diversity of riches or natural rarities; for almost all the objects which men who have ever been blessed by fortune have acquired one by one—the wonderful and precious productions of various nations—by their collective exhibition on that day displayed the majesty of the Roman empire. Silver and gold and ivory in masses, wrought into all manner of forms, might be seen, not as if carried in procession, but flowing, so to speak, like a river; here were tapestries borne along, some of the rarest purple, others embroidered by Babylonian art with perfect portraiture; transparent gems, some set in golden crowns, some in other fashions, swept by in such profusion as to correct our erroneous supposition that any of them was rare. Then, too, there were carried images of their gods, of marvelous size and no mean craftsmanship, and of these not one but was of some rich material. Beasts of many species were led along all caparisoned with appropriate trappings. The numerous attendants conducting each group of animals were decked in garments of true purple dye, interwoven with gold; while those selected to take part in the pageant itself had about them choice ornaments of amazing richness. Moreover, even among the mob or captives, none was to be seen unadorned, the variety and beauty of their dresses concealing from view any unsightliness arising from bodily disfigurement.

But nothing in the procession excited so much astonishment as the structure of the moving stages; indeed, their massiveness afforded ground for alarm and misgiving as to their stability, many of them being three or four stories high, while the magnificence of the fabric was a source at once of delight and amazement. For many were enveloped in tapestries interwoven with gold, and all had a framework of gold and wrought ivory. The war was shown by numerous representations, in separate sections, affording a very vivid picture of its episodes. Here was to be seen a prosperous country devastated, there whole battalions of the enemy slaughtered; here a party in flight, there others led into captivity; walls of surpassing compass demolished by engines, strong fortresses overpowered, cities with well-manned defenses completely mastered and an army pouring within the ramparts, an area all deluged with blood, the hands of those incapable of resistance raised in supplication, temples set on fire, houses pulled down over their owners' heads, and, after general desolation and woe, rivers flowing, not over a cultivated land, nor supplying drink to man and beast, but across a country still on every side in flames. For to such sufferings were the Jews destined when they plunged into war; and the art and magnificent workmanship of these structures now portrayed the incidents to those who had not witnessed them, as though they were happening before their eyes. On each of the stages was stationed the general of one of the captured cities in the attitude in which he was taken. A number of ships also followed.

The spoils in general were borne in promiscuous heaps; but conspicuous above all stood out those captured in the temple at Jerusalem. These consisted of a golden table, many talents in weight, and a lampstand likewise made of gold, but constructed on a different pattern from those which we use in ordinary life. Affixed to a pedestal was a central shaft, from which there extended slender branches, arranged trident fashion, a wrought lamp being attached to the extremity of each branch; of these were seven, indicating the honor paid to that number among the Jews. After these, and last of all the spoils, was carried a copy of the Jewish Law. Then followed a large party carrying images of victory, all made of ivory and gold. Behind them drove Vespasian, followed by Titus; while Domitian rode beside them, in magnificent apparel and mounted on a steed that was itself a sight.

6. The triumphal procession ended at the temple of Jupiter Capitolinus, on reaching which they halted; for it was a time-honored custom to wait there until the execution of the enemy's general was announced. This was Simon, son of Gioras, who had just figured in the pageant among the prisoners, and then, with a halter thrown over him and scourged meanwhile by his conductors, had been haled to the spot abutting on the Forum, where Roman law

requires that malefactors condemned to death should be executed. After the announcement that Simon was no more and the shouts of universal applause which greeted it, the princes began the sacrifices, which having been duly offered with the customary prayers, they withdrew to the palace. Some they entertained at a feast at their own table: for all the rest provision had already been made for banquets in their several homes. For the city of Rome kept festival that day for her victory in the campaign against her enemies, for the termination of her civil dissensions, and for the dawning hopes of felicity.

7. The triumphal ceremonies being concluded and the empire of the Romans established on the firmest foundation, Vespasian decided to erect a temple of Peace. This was very speedily completed and in a style surpassing all human conception. For, besides having prodigious resources of wealth on which to draw he also embellished it with ancient masterpieces of painting and sculpture; indeed, into that shrine were accumulated and stored all objects for the sight of which men had once wandered over the whole world, eager to see them severally while they lay in various countries. Here, too, he laid up the vessels of gold from the temple of the Jews, on which he prided himself; but their Law and the purple hangings of the sanctuary he ordered to be deposited and kept in the palace.[12]

Such is Josephus' account of the triumphal procession, which by that time Romans had been doing for centuries. One has the image of something like a modern-day parade with floats, but rather than showcasing the local Kiwanis club or square dancers, the Roman triumphal procession depicted scenes of battle complete with captured enemy units, generals, the populace, their wealth, and their sacred items, including the menorah, and the Scriptures (the Jewish Law)! We might also imagine the jeering faced by those literally put on parade. And in a final demonstration of Roman might and power, the leader of the defeated people is brought up to the Capitoline hill before the Temple of Jupiter Optimus Maximus (Jupiter the Best, the Greatest) and beheaded. In this case Simon bar Giora played that infamous role. For the Romans this was a celebration of their superiority, regardless of the enemy. These triumphal processions would have happened with some regularity so that the Roman people were reminded of their power and dominance. When Rome could defeat a people and display their leaders and symbols of power and wealth in a triumphal procession, it

12. Josephus, *The Jewish War* 7.5.3–7 in Thackeray, trans., *The Jewish War*.

demonstrated clearly that they, their way of life, their gods, their laws, their military were in all ways superior to the defeated enemy. This particular triumph, the same described by Josephus above, is depicted in relief on the Arch of Titus. As we approach it from the forum, we can see on the right panel the menorah.

and on the left panel the victors of the triumph:

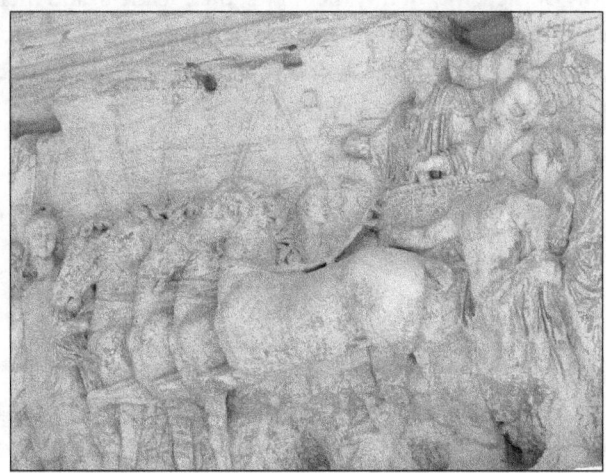

The inscription on the west side of the arch reads in Latin:

INSIGNE RELIGIONIS ATQVE ARTIS MONVMENTVM
VETVSTATE PATISCENS PIUS SEPTIMUS PONTIFEX MAX

NOVIS OPERIBUS PRISCUM EXEMPLAR IMITANTIBUS
FVLCIRI SERVARIQVE IVSSIT ANNO SACRI PRINCIPATVS
EIVS XXIIII

(This) monument, remarkable for its religion and its art, had weakened by age: Pius VII, Supreme Pontiff, by new works on the model of the ancient exemplar ordered it to be reinforced and saved in the 24th year of his sacred principate [i.e., 1823].

The inscription on the east side of the arch reads in Latin:

SENATUS POPULUSQUE ROMANUS DIVO TITO DIVI VES-
PASIANI F(ILIO) VESPASIANO AUGUSTO

The Senate and the Roman People (made this) for deified Titus Vespasian Augustus the son of deified Vespasian.

This monument reminds us of the destruction of Jerusalem and its Temple, and the significance this destruction had not only for the Jews, but also for the Romans, who commemorated the event with this arch. From the Roman point of view, the victory was a demonstration of their superiority and the superiority of their gods, especially Jupiter Optimus Maximus. The Roman ability to utterly destroy the Temple of Yahweh and raze Jerusalem to the ground demonstrated the superiority not only of their military, but primarily of their way of life, their laws, their leaders, and their gods. If there were any doubt, look no further than to this monumental arch depicting the sacred relics of the Jerusalem Temple. Rome is victorious over all.

Arch of Constantine

In the year 312 CE the leadership of the Roman Empire was in something of disarray. About twenty years prior, Diocletian had divided the empire into East and West to facilitate more effective governance. He also established the tetrarchy, or four-man rule. There were to be two *Augusti* (himself in the East and Maximian in the West). Below each *Augustus* there was a *Caesar*, thus the four man rule, the tetrarchy. Diocletian's Caesar was Galerius; whereas Maximian's Caesar was Constantius. Both Diocletian and Maximian abdicated in 305, whereupon civil war shortly ensued with various generals, tetrarchs, sons of emperors and others being named emperor.

As part of the internal power struggle of the early fourth century, Constantine (son of Constantius, who had died in 306 of natural causes) was vying for control of the Western Empire against the forces of Maxentius (son of Maximian). Moreover, Constantine and Maxentius were brothers-in-law, as Constantine had married Maximian's daughter Flavia Maxima Fausta. Maxentius was safely ensconced in the fortified city of Rome when Constantine, marched his army through Italy to attack. It was about this time that Constantine had his most famous vision.

Eusebius, a contemporary and friend of Constantine, relates the story in this way, expressing his own hesitation about the fantastical elements told to him:

> As he [Constantine] made these prayers and earnest supplications there appeared to the Emperor a most remarkable divine sign. If

someone else had reported it, it would perhaps not be easy [30] to accept; but since the victorious emperor himself told the story to the present writer a long while after, when I was privileged with his acquaintance and company, and confirmed it with oaths, who could hesitate to believe the account, especially when the time which followed provided evidence for the truth of what he said? (2) About the time of the midday sun, when the day was just turning, he said he saw with his own eyes, up in the sky and resting over the sun, a cross-shaped trophy formed from light, and a text attached to it which said, 'By this conquer'. Amazement at the spectacle seized both him and the whole company of soldiers which was then accompanying him on a campaign he was conducting somewhere, and witnessed the miracle.

29 He was, he said, wondering to himself what the manifestation might mean; then, while he meditated, and though long and hard, night overtook him. Thereupon, as he slept, the Christ of God appeared to him with the sign which had appeared in the sky, and urged him to make himself a copy of the sign which had appeared in the sky, and to use this as protection against the attacks of the enemy. 30 When day came he arose and recounted the mysterious communication to his friends. Then he summoned goldsmiths and jewelers, sat down among them, and explained the shape of the sign, and gave them instructions about copying it in gold and precious stones.

This was something which the Emperor himself once saw fit to let me also set eyes on, God vouchsafing even this. 31 (1) It was constructed to the following design. A tall pole plated with gold had a transverse bar forming the shape of a cross. Up at [31] the extreme top a wreath woven of precious stones and gold had been fastened. On it two letters, intimating by its first characters the name 'Christ', formed the monogram of the Saviour's title, *rho* [P] being intersected in the middle by *chi* [X]. These letters the Emperor also used to wear upon his helmet in later times ... (3) This saving sign was always used by the Emperor for protection against every opposing and hostile force, and he commanded replicas of it to lead all his armies.

32 (1) That was, however, somewhat later. At the time in question, stunned by the amazing vision, and determined to worship no other god than the one who had appeared, he summoned those expert in his words, and enquired who this god was, and what was the explanation of the vision which had appeared of the sign. (2) They said that the god was the Onlybegotten Son of the one and only God, and that the sign which appeared was a token of

immortality, and was an abiding trophy of the victory over death, which he had won once when he was present on earth. They began to teach him the reasons for his coming, explaining to him in detail the story of his self-accommodation to human conditions. [32] (3) He listened attentively to these accounts too, while he marveled at the divine manifestation which had been granted to his eyes; comparing the heavenly vision with the meaning of what was being said, he made up his mind, convinced that it was as God's own teaching that the knowledge of these things had come to him. He now decided personally to apply himself to the divinely inspired writing. Taking the priests of God as his advisers, he also deemed it right to honour the God who had appeared to him with all due rites. Thereafter, fortified by good hopes in him, he finally set about extinguishing the menacing flames of tyranny.[13]

And with that Eusebius continues his story with the campaign of Constantine against Maxentius.

Maxentius made the strategic and fatal error of leading his forces outside the heavily fortified city to meet Constantine's army at the Milvian bridge, just a few miles north of the city.[14] Indeed the forces of Constantine won the battle, and eventually (in 324) the empire, both East and West. One year after the Battle of the Milvian Bridge Constantine issued the Edict of Milan. The edict in effect legitimized Christianity, though it was not yet the official religion of the empire. Constantine eventually moved the seat of the empire to Byzantium in the East, and renamed it Constantinople.

The Arch of Constantine commemorates his victory over Maxentius with these words. Note the reference to a divinity.

IMP[ERATORI] CAES[ARI] FL[AVIO] CONSTANTINO
MAXIMO
P[IO] F[ELICI] AVGVSTO S[ENATVS] P[OPVLVS]Q[VE]
R[OMANVS]
QVOD INSTINCTV DIVINITATIS MENTIS
MAGNITVDINE CVM EXERCITV SVO
TAM DE TYRANNO QVAM DE OMNI EIVS
FACTIONE VNO TEMPORE IVSTIS
REMPVBLICAM VLTVS EST ARMIS
ARCVM TRIVMPHIS INSIGNEM DICAVIT

13. Eusebius, *Life of Constantine*, I. 28–32.
14. In antiquity the Milvian bridge was just outside Rome. Today Rome has grown around it and it is considered within the city. The bridge carries the Via Flaminia across the Tiber.

THE ROME OF PETER AND PAUL—PART II

> To the Emperor Caesar Flavius Constantine, the Greatest,
> Pius, Felix Augustus:
> because inspired by (a) divinity, and by the greatness of his mind,
> with his army and just force of arms, at one [and the same] time
> he delivered the state from a tyrant on the one hand and every
> kind of factionalism on the other;
> therefore the Senate and the People of Rome
> have dedicated this exceptional arch to his triumphs.

Scholars and historians have debated the meaning of Constantine's phrase, INSTINCTU DIVINITATIS (inspired by a divinity) ever since the arch was erected. There simply is not explicit reference to God, much less a Christian God, or even Jesus Christ. As a result, some claim that Constantine was still not fully committed to Christianity. Others say that he was acting as a shrewd politician, giving credit not only to a divinity, but also to the greatness of his own mind. Whatever the case may be, these two words are the only clue we have on this monument that Constantine attributed his victory (at least partially) to the inspiration of God.

Students and perceptive observers often ask about the other inscriptions that can be seen easily on the monument: VOTIS X, SIC X, SIC XX, etc. commemorate the tenth and twentieth anniversaries of his reign (315 and 325 respectively). It seems Constantine was in Rome for the tenth anniversary and perhaps the twentieth. If so, these would have been the only times he returned to Rome after he conquered the city and Maxentius, for he moved the capital city to the newly named, "Constantinople." What Nero had in mind, naming a capital city for himself, Constantine did, though it was not Rome. Rather, by the time of Constantine, Rome seems to have traveled a great distance along the long and winding path to decline.

Finally, as to other inscriptions, we also read on the inside of the central archway: LIBERATORI VRBIS (liberator of the city)—FUNDATORI QVIETIS (founder of peace). We might be reminded of the Roman saying, "they create desolation and call it peace." The people of Rome are to be reminded that Constantine's victory over Maxentius was "liberation" as Constantine himself brought "peace." And here we see, combined with the earlier mention of "inspired by a divinity," what a master politician Constantine was. This is imperial propaganda pure and simple. There was certainly no TV, Facebook, or hashtags to promote his agenda. But that purpose was accomplished by this imposing arch with its inscriptions. His messaging campaign appears worthy of emulation by modern politicians.

Apart from the matter of the inscriptions, we must also notice the haphazard way in which the monument is decorated. In fact, all but a few elements have been imported from previous pagan monuments. In other words, only the reliefs immediately above the smaller arches, as well as the winged victories and captives at the base were made specifically for this arch. The statues of men standing atop are Thracians from the monument of Trajan. The life of Marcus Aurelius is depicted in the eight rectangular reliefs. The eight large medallions that depict hunting scenes come from the time of Hadrian.

Constantine plundered these other monuments in making his own because the knowledge and execution of the arts in Rome had diminished. This is also part of the reason Constantine moves the seat of the empire from Rome. By the early fourth century Rome was already in a state of decline. See for yourself the quality of the artisans of the Constantinian era by comparing the reliefs above the arches with the roundels from Hadrian's time, or the other pagan elements present.

Ultimately, the arch of Constantine symbolizes more than the victory at the Milvian bridge. By incorporating pagan elements in its architecture, and by only begrudgingly sharing credit for the victory with a divine impetus, the arch strangely commemorates the human will to power, fame, and selfishness. The arch is in Rome, which no longer holds the seat of power for the empire. Constantine claims the victory is not only due to divinity but also his own great mind. To commemorate this event fine artisans are not hired (because they are not available?) and instead other works are plundered. The arch also stands then as a gateway between the classical era and the Christian era.

Colosseum

Quandiu stat Colisaeus, stat et Roma;
quando cadet Colisaeus, cadet et Roma.
Quando cadet Roma, cadet et mundus.[15]

As long as the Colisaeus stands, so Rome stands;
When the Colisaeus falls, Rome falls too.
When Rome falls, the world falls too.

This verse of Pseudo-Bede is often applied to the Colosseum. In truth, the term Colisaeus is a reference to the 106-foot statue that Nero erected near his lake, after the great fire of 64 CE. The Roman historian Suetonius describes palatial estate with its colossal statue.

> There was nothing however in which he was more ruinously prodigal than in building. He made a palace extending all the way from the Palatine to the Esquiline, which at first he called the House of Passage, but when it was burned shortly after its completion and rebuilt, the Golden House. Its size and splendour will be sufficiently indicated by the following details. Its vestibule was large enough to contain a colossal statue of the emperor a hundred and twenty feet high; and it was so extensive that it had a triple colonnade a mile long. There was a pond too, like a sea, surrounded with

---

15. Pseudo-Bede, "Excerptiones Patrum, Collectanea, Flores Ex Diversis, Quaestiones, Et Parabolae," in *PL*, 94.543B.

buildings to represent cities, besides tracts of country, varied by tilled fields, vineyards, pastures and woods, with great numbers of wild and domestic animals. In the rest of the house all parts were overlaid with gold and adorned with gems and mother-of-pearl. There were dining-rooms with fretted ceilings of ivory, whose panels could turn and shower down flowers and were fitted with pipes for sprinkling the guests with perfumes. The main banquet hall was circular and constantly revolved day and night, like the heavens. He had baths supplied with sea water and sulphur water. When the edifice was finished in this style and he dedicated it, he deigned to say nothing more in the way of approval than that he was at last beginning to be housed like a human being.[16]

When Vespasian Flavius became emperor, he drained the lake in order to create an amphitheater for the people. The Colisaeus stood nearby until the Middle Ages. Thus the Flavian amphitheater was also known (from medieval times) as the Colosseum. Though, it is important to remember that the ancient Romans would have called it simply the arena, the hunting-theater, or the Flavian amphitheater.

Vespasian died in 79 CE, one year before the grand opening of the amphitheater under the emperor Titus, son of Vespasian. The poet Martial wrote verses to commemorate the opening of the Flavian amphitheater. Perhaps Martial captures the sentiments of the people best with this verse:

> Where the starry colossus sees the constellations at close range
> and lofty scaffolding rises in the middle of the road,
> once gleamed the odious halls of a cruel monarch,
> and in all Rome there stood a single house.
> Where the rises before our eyes the august pile of the Amphitheater,
> once was Nero's lake.
> Where we admire the warm baths, a speedy gift,
> a haughty tract of land had robbed the poor of their dwellings.
> Where the Claudian colonnade unfolds its wide-spread shade,
> was the outermost part of the palace's end.
> Rome has been restored to herself, and under your rule, Caesar,
> the pleasances that belonged to a master now belong to the people.[17]

---

16. Suetonius, *Nero*, 15, in *Lives of the Caesars*.
17. Martial, *Spectacles*, 2 in *Epigrams I*, 13, 15.

We read earlier how Vespasian gave Nero's lake and palace back to the people in the form of an amphitheater. The opening of the amphitheater was celebrated not only in celebratory verse but in celebratory carnage. Cassius Dio, the Roman historian writing more than one hundred years after the event, describes the grand opening this way:

> Most that he did was not characterized by anything noteworthy, but in dedicating the hunting-theatre and the baths that bear his name he produced many remarkable spectacles.
>
> There was a battle between cranes and also between four elephants; animals both tame and wild were slain to the number of nine thousand; and women (not those of any prominence, however) took part in dispatching them. As for the men, several fought in single combat and several groups contended together both in infantry and naval battles. For Titus suddenly filled this same theatre with water and brought in horses and bulls and some other domesticated animals that had been taught to behave in the liquid element just as on land. He also brought in people on ships, who engaged in a sea-fight there, impersonating the Corcyreans and Corinthians; and others gave a similar exhibition outside the city in the grove of Gaius and Lucius, a place which Augustus had once excavated for this very purpose.
>
> There, too, on the first day there was a gladiatorial exhibition and wild-beast hunt, the lake in front of the images having first been covered over with a platform of planks and wooden stands erected around it. On the second day there was a horse-race, and on the third day a naval battle between three thousand men, followed by an infantry battle. The "Athenians" conquered the "Syracusans" (these were the names the combatants used), made a landing on the islet and assaulted and captured a wall that had been constructed around the monument. These were the spectacles that were offered, and they continued for a hundred days; but Titus also furnished some things that were of practical use to the people.
>
> He would throw down into the theatre from aloft little wooden balls variously inscribed, one designating some article of food, another clothing, another a silver vessel or perhaps a gold one, or again horses, pack-animals, cattle or slaves. Those who seized them were to carry them to the dispensers of the bounty, from whom they would receive the article named.
>
> After he had finished these exhibitions, and had wept so bitterly on the last day that all the people saw him, he performed no other deed of importance; but the next day, in the consulship of

Flavius and Pollio, after the dedication of the buildings mentioned, he passed away at the same watering-place that had been the scene of his father's death. [18]

From Dio's account, the games at the Colosseum seem in many ways similar to our own sporting events with prizes for ticket holders. Yet, in many more ways the games were different. For the most part, primarily men attended. There were some women there (the Vestal Virgins had seats next to the Emperor); common women could sit in the fourth tier (the highest).

The ancient games were different from our own in another way too. Thousands of beasts were killed. We wonder what a battle between cranes and another between elephants would have been like.

The amphitheater was built in part to quench the bloodthirst of the Romans. Gladiatorial combat and games of death did not begin with the amphitheater, but were quite popular with the people before the Colosseum was constructed. In this letter from Seneca the Younger (4 BCE– 65 CE) to Lucilius we hear a condemnation of the games. But remember, this was written before the amphitheater was built. Seneca thus speaks of games that were held in a temporary theater to celebrate some event.

> But nothing is so damaging to good character as the habit of lounging at the games; for then it is that vice steals subtly upon one through the avenue of pleasure. What do you think I mean? I mean that I come home more greedy, more ambitious, more voluptuous, and even more cruel and inhuman, — because I have been among human beings. By chance I attended a mid-day exhibition, expecting some fun, wit, and relaxation,—an exhibition at which men's eyes have respite from the slaughter of their fellow-men. But it was quite the reverse. The previous combats were the essence of compassion; but now all the trifling is put aside and it is pure murder. The men have no defensive armour. They are exposed to blows at all points, and no one ever strikes in-vain. Many persons prefer this programme to the usual pairs and to the bouts "by request." Of course they do; there is no helmet or shield to deflect the weapon. What is the need of defensive armour, or of skill? All these mean delaying death. In the morning they throw men to the lions and the bears; at noon, they throw them to the spectators. The spectators demand that the slayer shall face the man who is to slay him in his turn; and they always reserve the latest conqueror

---

18. Cassius Dio, "Epitome of Book LXVI," in *Roman History*, 66.25a–26.1b.

for another butchering. The outcome of every fight is death, and the means are fire and sword. This sort of thing goes on while the arena is empty. You may retort: "But he was a highway robber; he killed a man!" And what of it? Granted that, as a murderer, he deserved this punishment, what crime have you committed, poor fellow, that you should deserve to sit and see this show? In the morning they cried "Kill him! Lash him! Burn him! Why does he meet the sword in so cowardly a way? Why does he strike so feebly? Why doesn't he die game? Whip him to meet his wounds! Let them receive blow for blow, with chests bare and exposed to the stroke!" And when the games stop for the intermission, they announce: "A little throat-cutting in the meantime, so that there may still be something going on!"[19]

Yet, the Romans did not take Seneca's advice and as we have seen, the Flavian Amphitheater became a central feature of the Roman entertainment landscape. Martial, the Roman poet commissioned to commemorate the opening of the games with verse, knew that the amphitheater was something grand:

> Let barbarous Memphis speak no more of the wonder
>   of her pyramids,
>
> nor Assyrian toil boast of Babylon;
>
> nor let the soft Ionians be extolled for Triva's temple;
>
> let the altar of the many horns say naught of Delos;
>
> nor let the Carians exalt to the skies with extravagant
>   praises the Mausoleum
>
>   poised in the empty air.
>
> All labor yields to Caesar's Amphitheater.
>
> Fame shall tell of one work in lieu of all.[20]

Besides verse to commemorate the grandeur of the monument, Martial also tells us something of the games that went on in the arena. Some of these games were a means of capital punishment. That is, Romans dealt with murderers by murdering them publicly. Often they enacted certain myths in the arena. As Seneca deplored this aspect of the games, Martial revels in it:

---

19. Seneca, *Epistles*, 7.3–5.
20. Martial, *Spectacles*, 1 in *Epigrams I*, 13.

As Prometheus, bound on Scythian crag,
> fed the tireless bird with his too abundant breast,

so did Laureolus, hanging on no sham cross,
> give his naked flesh to a Caledonian boar.

His lacerated limbs lived on, dripping gore,
> and all in all his body, body there was none.

Finally he met with the punishment he deserved;
> the guilty wretch had plunged a sword into his father's throat
>
> or his master's, or in his madness had robbed a temple of its secret gold,
>
> or laid a cruel torch to Rome.

The criminal had outdone the misdeeds of ancient story;
> in him, what had been a play had become an execution.[21]

In the myth, Prometheus was chained to a rock and each morning a bird would arrive to eat his liver, which would grow back for the next day. Zeus inflicted this punishment on Prometheus because Prometheus had given humanity fire. The Romans thought it fun to re-enact this myth with a condemned criminal, fastened to a cross. We can image an "announcer" calling out to the crowd the name of the condemned criminal, and the myth that would be reenacted. Then rising up from a trap door the animal would appear, as Martial again informs us: "Earth through a sudden opening sent a bear to attack Orpheus. She came from Eurydice."[22]

Besides executing criminals, the arena was also a place to watch different animals fight each other. At times, the animals did not immediately attack. We can imagine the crowd booing, or jeering, with animal trainers/handlers attempting to prod the creatures into conflict. For example,

> While the trembling trainers were goading the rhinoceros and the great beast's anger was long a-gathering, men were giving up hope of the combats of promised warfare; but at length the fury we earlier knew returned. For with his double horn he tossed a heavy bear as a bull tosses dummies from his head to the stars. [With how sure a stroke does the strong hand of Carpophorus, still a youth, aim Norican spears!] He lifted two steers with his mobile

21. Ibid., 9.
22. Ibid., 25.

neck, to him yielded the fierce buffalo and the bison. A lion fleeing before him ran headlong upon the spears. Go now, you crowd, complain of tedious delays![23]

The Romans also thought it interesting to combine different animals in the arena to see what might happen. In one battle they might pit a rhinoceros against a bull; in another, a bull against an elephant.

> The rhinoceros, displayed all over the arena, performed for you, Caesar, battles that he did not promise. How he lowered his head and flamed into fearful rage! How mighty a bull was he, to whom a bull was as a dummy![24]

> The bull, that goaded with fire through the whole arena had just snatched up dummies and tossed them to the stars, at length met his death, trampled by a horned mouth. He thought it would be easy to toss an elephant so.[25]

Besides executions, and wild beasts facing each other, at times Caesar would show his prowess in the arena, throwing spears at animals. This was not so much an exercise of courage as skill in accuracy and precision. The animals were deer, rabbits, or even pigs. One particularly gruesome and bizarre event sparked Martial to write three verses:

> Amid the cruel perils of Caesar's hunt a light spear had pierced a pregnant sow. One of her litter lept out of hapless mother's wound. Savage Lucina, was *this* a delivery? She would have wished to die wounded by further weapons, so that the sad path might open for all her brood. Who denies that Bacchus sprang from his mother's death? Believe that a deity was so given birth: so born was a beast.[26]

> A mother sow, struck by a heavy weapon and laid open by the wound, lost life and gave it at one and the same time. How sure was the hand that poised the steel! I believe this hand was Lucina's. Dying, the creature sampled the divine power of either Diana. By one the parent was delivered, by the other the beast was slain.[27]

23. Ibid., 26.
24. Ibid., 11.
25. Ibid., 22.
26. Ibid., 14.
27. Ibid., 15.

A wild sow, now pregnant, sent forth her progeny, pledge of her ripe womb, made parent by a wound. Nor did the offspring lie on the ground, but ran as the mother fell. How ingenious are sudden chances![28]

Thus provides a sense of the games openings. Thousands of beasts killed, gladiatorial combats, criminal executions, free food, and prizes. This attracted the ancient Roman male for centuries.

Augustine too relates a story of a young man whom he knew in North Africa, Alypius. While there Alypius was entranced by the games to such a degree that he nearly wasted his intellectual talent on them. Instead, after hearing a lecture by Augustine, Alypius forsook the games. From here the story is told in Augustine's own voice:

> He certainly did not abandon that earthly course which his parents had dinned into him. He had made his way to Rome to learn law, and it was there that he was extraordinarily carried away by this extraordinary appetite for gladiatorial shows. For although he disliked and detested them, he happened to bump into some friends and fellow students on their way back from a dinner, and they used friendly force to drag him, still hotly protesting and resisting, into the amphitheater at a time when the deadly and cruel shows were taking place. He declared, "You may drag my body to such a place and set it down there, but surely you cannot also fix my mind and gaze upon those performances? I shall be both present, and absent: and so I will defeat both you and them." His friends listened, then took him along with them just the same, perhaps because they were eager to test that precise point, whether he could succeed.
>
> When they arrived there and settled into what seats they could, everything was a hotbed of monstrous gratification. He closed his eyes as a point of access, and forbade his mind to step forth into such evils. If only he had closed his ears likewise! For at one fall in a fight a loud roar from the whole crowd struck him with full force; he was overcome with curiosity and like someone prepared to condemn and subdue what he saw, whatever it might be, he opened his eyes. At once he was struck by a wound to his soul that was deeper than the wound the combatant he was now eager to watch suffered to his body. He sank down, more pitiable than the man whose fall had given rise to the shouting. That noise entered into his ears and unlocked his eyes, to make a way for

---

28. Ibid., 16.

the striking down and subjugation of a mind that up to this point had been confident rather than courageous, and all the weaker for relying on itself when it should have relied on you. For when he saw that blood, he drank deep of its barbarity and did not turn himself away but fixed his gaze and drank in the torments and was unaware, and found gratification in the wickedness of the contest, and became drunk on the pleasures of blood. Now he was no longer the same person as when he had come. He was one of the crowd that he had joined, a true companion of the friends who had taken him there. Why say any more? He watched, he shouted, he burned; he took with him from that place the madness that goaded him to return, not just with those friends who had first carried him away but even more before them, and taking others along. And yet you rescued him from there with a mighty and merciful hand, and you taught him to put his trust in you and not in himself. But that only happened much later."[29]

By the time of the twelfth century, the Romans had quite literally forgotten their heritage for the *Mirabilia* states quite forthrightly, "The Colosseum was the Temple of the Sun."[30]

When we see the Colosseum today we may be reminded of the many stories of Christian martyrdom that are legendary. It is interesting to note however, that there is no primary evidence that indicates that Christians were killed in the Colosseum. Be that as it may, the legend of Ignatius of Antioch (d. 107 CE) is strong. It seems that he was preparing for death at the jaws of the lions. Whether that took place in the Colosseum or not is anybody's guess. Yet, tradition places his martyrdom there and we call to mind the fact that for the Romans, this would have been just another executed criminal, one who received what he had coming. The fact that they did not record his name is not surprising. The legend that his remains are at San Clemente allows us to imagine the pious Christians picking up his bones and torn flesh from the arena, and taking them to the house of Flavius Clemens, residence too of Clement of Rome. If it seems too fantastic, it is the matter of romance. If it seems possible, perhaps you are a romantic!

Ignatius seems to prepare himself mentally and spiritually for what awaits him in Rome in this letter to the Romans:

> I am writing all the churches and giving instruction to all, that I am willingly dying for God, unless you hinder me. I urge you, do

---

29. Augustine, *Confessions*, 6.8.
30. Gardiner, *Marvels of Rome*, 28 (2.7).

not become an untimely kindness to me. Allow me to be bread for the wild beasts; through them I am able to attain to God. I am the wheat of God and am ground by the teeth of the wild beasts, that I may be found to be the pure bread of Christ.

Rather, coax the wild beasts, that they may become a tomb for me and leave no part of my body behind, that I may burden no one once I have died. Then I will truly be a disciple of Jesus Christ, when the world does not see even my body. Petition Christ on my behalf, that I may be found a sacrifice through these instruments of God.

I am not enjoining you as Peter and Paul did. They were apostles, I am condemned; they were free, until now I have been a slave. But if I suffer, I will become a freed person who belongs to Jesus Christ, and I will rise up, free, in him. In the meantime I am learning to desire nothing while in chains.[31]

As we stand in and around the Colosseum we see it as a monument to Rome, its depravity and its architectural brilliance. As we ponder its arches, its symmetry, the monument to theatrical and vicious combat, what does it say about the ancient Romans? What does it say about the human spirit? Ultimately, as it still stands, what does it say about us?

As we walk from the Colosseum to San Clemente on the Via S. Giovanni in Laterano, look to your left to see excavations of the Ludus Magnus (Big Camp). These are the remains of one of the most famous gladiatorial training camps. In antiquity there was an underground tunnel from this camp to below the arena at the Colosseum.

Santa Prisca (and Aquila)

Prisca (a.k.a. Priscilla) and Aquila were important and prominent Jewish Christians, contemporaries and friends of Paul. They are mentioned by him in 1 Cor 16:19 and Rom 16:3–5. They are also mentioned by Luke in Acts 18:1–3, 18, 26 (where Priscilla is the name used) and they are named in 2 Tim 4:19. The name Prisca was not typically a slave name, leading scholars to believe she was born free. Moreover, she is usually listed first, before her husband, lending more credibility to the thought that she was well-educated, prominent in her own right, and perhaps had means. Aquila, a Jewish tentmaker from Pontus (Northeast Asia Minor on the Black Sea), was her husband and together they lived as Jewish Christians in Rome. In

---

31. Ignatius of Antioch, *Letter to the Romans*, 4.

49 CE, when Claudius expelled the Jews from Rome, Prisca and Aquila left for Corinth, where they met Paul for the first time. He stayed with them for about two years before they all travelled to Ephesus together, according to Acts.

> After this he [Paul] left Athens and went to Corinth. There he met a Jew named Aquila, a native of Pontus, who had recently come from Italy with his wife Priscilla because Claudius had ordered all the Jews to leave Rome. He went to visit them and, because he practiced the same trade, stayed with them and worked, for they were tentmakers by trade (Acts 18:1–3).

> Paul remained for quite some time, and after saying farewell to the brothers he sailed for Syria, together with Priscilla and Aquila. At Cenchreae he had his hair cut because he had taken a vow. When they reached Ephesus, he left them there, while he entered the synagogue and held discussions with the Jews. Although they asked him to stay for a longer time, he did not consent, but as he said farewell he promised, "I shall come back to you again, God willing." Then he set sail from Ephesus (Acts 18:18–21).

It was in Ephesus that Prisca and Aquila hosted the church at their home: "The churches of Asia send you greetings. Aquila and Prisca together with the church at their house send you many greetings in the Lord." (1 Cor 16:19). And it was in Ephesus that Prisca and Aquila instructed Apollos more accurately in "The Way" (Christianity) as Apollos had only known the baptism of John (Acts 18:25–26). And finally, it seems that by the time Paul wrote Romans (winter of 57–58), the Jews had been allowed to return to Rome. Prisca and Aquila had re-established their home there, which had already become a meeting place for the church. So Paul greets Prisca and Aquila by name, and expresses gratitude for their courage.

> Greet Prisca and Aquila, my co-workers in Christ Jesus, who risked their necks for my life, to whom not only I am grateful but also all the churches of the Gentiles; greet also the church at their house (Rom 16:3–5).

Thus this prominent Jewish-Christian married couple were instrumental in the growth and development of apostolic Christianity. They likely heard about Jesus while in Rome, sometime prior to 49, i.e., prior to Peter or Paul's arrival there. Being expelled from the city, they moved to Corinth where they met and hosted Paul. We can only imagine the conversations that must have taken place during those two years in Corinth where they practiced their mutual trade, and shared stories about Jesus and his significance. It was during this time in Corinth that Paul was manhandled by the proconsul Gallio,[32] and we can only presume what Paul was referring to when he later says that Prisca and Aquila "risked their necks" for him. Prisca and Aquila knew and enjoyed Paul so well that they even travelled together (which is more than we can say for other New Testament characters! Cf. the story of Barnabas, Acts 15:36–41). They remained in Ephesus coming to know other prominent Christians of the time including the charismatic Apollos. In fact, they were so well-versed in "The Way" that they felt comfortable instructing the popular preacher. Once the emperor Claudius died and the young Nero took the purple, it seems the ban on Jews in Rome was lifted, which allowed Prisca and Aquila to return. When they did, they established a house-church as they had done in Ephesus, so that when Paul wrote his letter to the Romans he specifically mentions them.

By the fourth century, the legendary site of their home on the Aventine, an upper-middle class neighborhood in antiquity and even today, was built a church, *titulus Priscae*. There are also catacombs that bear her name though a historical link is dubious.

The church has little architectural detail to commend it. Aside from its legendary association with Prisca and Aquila, it is perhaps best known for sitting atop an ancient Mithraeum, better preserved than the one at San Clemente. One can visit this Mithraeum from the right nave of the church, but only on the second and fourth Sunday of each month at 4 p.m.![33]

---

32. Gallio happened to be the son of Seneca the Elder, and the older brother of Seneca the Younger. Gallio did not enjoy his limited time in Corinth. He developed a fever soon after arriving, and departed shortly thereafter, insisting that the disease was not of the body but of the place! (Seneca, *Epistles*, 104.1–2).

33. http://archeoroma.beniculturali.it/en/archaeological-site/mithraeum-st-prisca

St. Peter in Chains
(San Pietro in Vincoli)

Luke tells us in the Acts of the Apostles, that Peter was held in chains by Herod when in the middle of the night an angel rescued him and he escaped unharmed.

> About that time King Herod laid hands upon some members of the church to harm them. He had James, the brother of John, killed by the sword, and when he saw that this was pleasing to the Jews he proceeded to arrest Peter also. (It was [the] feast of Unleavened Bread.) He had him taken into custody and put in prison under the guard of four squads of four soldiers each. He intended to bring him before the people after Passover. Peter thus was being kept in prison, but prayer by the church was fervently being made to God on his behalf.
>
> On the very night before Herod was to bring him to trial, Peter, secured by double chains, was sleeping between two soldiers, while outside the door guards kept watch on the prison. Suddenly the angel of the Lord stood by him and a light shone in the cell. He tapped Peter on the side and awakened him, saying, "Get up quickly." The chains fell from his wrists. The angel said to him, "Put on your belt and your sandals." He did so. Then he said to him, "Put on your cloak and follow me." So he followed him out, not realizing that what was happening through the angel was real; he thought he was seeing a vision. They passed the first guard, then the second, and came to the iron gate leading out to the city, which opened for them by itself. They emerged and made their way down

an alley, and suddenly the angel left him. Then Peter recovered his senses and said, "Now I know for certain that [the] Lord sent his angel and rescued me from the hand of Herod and from all that the Jewish people had been expecting." When he realized this, he went to the house of Mary, the mother of John who is called Mark, where there were many people gathered in prayer. When he knocked on the gateway door, a maid named Rhoda came to answer it. She was so overjoyed when she recognized Peter's voice that, instead of opening the gate, she ran in and announced that Peter was standing at the gate. They told her, "You are out of your mind," but she insisted that it was so. But they kept saying, "It is his angel." But Peter continued to knock, and when they opened it, they saw him and were astounded. He motioned to them with his hand to be quiet and explained [to them] how the Lord had led him out of the prison, and said, "Report this to James and the brothers." Then he left and went to another place (Acts 12:1–17).

Though there are problems with the account, according to the twelfth-century *Mirabilia*, the church was founded by Eudoxia, widow of the Arcadius, Emperor of the East (r. 383–408), and mother of Theodosius II, Emperor of the East (r. 408–450). After Arcadius died, Theodosius was declared emperor of the East at the age of seven! Of course, it was Eudoxia who effectively ruled for her child. In so doing, she went to Jerusalem and visited various holy sites there. Many of the people in Judea brought her gifts, including one who brought her the chains of Peter from when he was imprisoned by Herod (Acts 12). According to the story, she pressed the Pope, the Senators and the People that a church should be constructed for these chains. As the people had been worshiping Octavian, Eudoxia implored them, "I pray you give up the worship of the dead Emperor Octavian for the worship of the heavenly Emperor and his Apostles Peter, whose chains, you see, I have brought from Jerusalem. Just as Octavian delivered us from Egyptian bondage [Cleopatra and Mark Antony], so did the heavenly Emperor deliver us from the bondage of demons. I intend to build a church to God's honor and to St. Peter's and to set these chains there." After some initial consternation the proposal was eventually accepted. Once the church was constructed, Eudoxia placed the chains of Peter there, and also the chains by which Nero bound Paul.[34]

The legend is rather fantastic, but explains the medieval understanding of the raison-d'etre for the church. Today most visitors find this place

---

34. Gardiner, *Marvels of Rome*, 26–28 (1.6).

of worship not because of the chains of Peter because of Michelangelo's Moses. This famous sculpture, made around 1514–1516 was to be part of Pope Julius II's tomb, which was itself to have over forty statues and be the most impressive funeral monument of all time. Instead, there was such vitriol over the work, which was envisioned as part of the renovated St. Peter's, that Michelangelo eventually abandoned it. Statues of two slaves that were intended for the final work are currently in the Louvre, and four unfinished statues of slaves are in the Accademia in Florence. This statue of Moses, and others made by Michelangelo's pupils, were moved to San Pietro in Vincoli in 1544 and have remained here ever since.[35] It seems poetic justice that Pope Julius II's most magnificent funeral monument in history was never completed and parts are scattered throughout Italy, with Michelangelo's Moses tucked away behind St. Peter's chains.

When one looks upon the statue, one sees immediately the horns on the head of Moses. These horns have been the source of never-ending debate. But essentially, the horns are from the Latin version of the Exodus story wherein Moses comes down from the mountain with the two tablets of the Decalogue. First, here is the NABRE version of the story with the pertinent section of the Latin Vulgate in parentheses:

> Then the LORD said to Moses: Write down these words, for in accordance with these words I have made a covenant with you and with Israel. So Moses was there with the LORD for forty days and forty nights, without eating any food or drinking any water, and he wrote on the tablets the words of the covenant, the ten words.
>
> As Moses came down from Mount Sinai with the two tablets of the covenant in his hands, he did not know that the skin of his face had become radiant (*et ignorabat quod cornuta esset facies sua*) while he spoke with the LORD. When Aaron, then, and the other Israelites saw Moses and noticed how radiant the skin of his face had become (*videntes autem Aaron et filii Israhel cornutam Mosi faciem*), they were afraid to come near him (Exod 34:27–30).

The key term in Latin is *cornuta(m)*, which means "bearing (or having) horns." This is a mistranslation of the Hebrew, which uses the term, "radiant." Even the notes in the NABRE indicate that: "the Hebrew word translated 'radiant' is spelled like the term for 'horns.' Thus the artistic tradition of portraying Moses with horns." Some art critics see the horns as an artistic representation of "rays of light." But we recall that Michelangelo

---

35. Masson, *Companion Guide to Rome*, 433.

would have been familiar with the Latin version of the Bible, and would have read the Latin term, "*cornuta*" as "bearing (or having) horns".

There are some interesting legends associated with this statue too. Michelangelo is said to have struck its knee with a hammer commanding it, "Speak!" If one looks closely a mark on the knee can be seen. The arms are criticized for being too large and out of proportion, but this may simply be Michelangelo's depiction of Moses in his prime.

The two statues on either side of Moses, Leah and Rachel, symbolizing the active and contemplative life, are also Michelangelo's work.

An interesting fact for those from the United States, is that S. Pietro in Vincoli is considered the titular church of Donald Cardinal Wuerl, Archbishop of Washington, D.C. A "titular" church, meaning a "title" church, is assigned to each cardinal. Historically, the *Liber Pontificalis* speaks of twenty-five titular churches, and the presbyters who presided over each were held in esteem. Today, when a bishop is named a cardinal he is assigned a titular church where he might preach when he is in Rome, or assist with its upkeep (by fundraising). But of course, the cardinal is not involved in the day-to-day management of his titular church.

Saint Clement
(San Clemente)

San Clemente is one of the most fascinating archeological sites of early Christianity in Rome. Here we have a twelfth-century church, built atop a fourth-century church, built atop a late first-century house, built atop the rubble from the great fire of Rome in 64 CE. During our tour we will see the "top" three layers. Also significant is that the first-century house is literally across the street, or next door, to a Mithraic cult room, which we shall also see.

The Church of Saint Clement (Basilica San Clemente) is named after the third Bishop of Rome, the purported author of 1 Clement. That letter sent by Clement to the church in Corinth was so influential and well regarded that is was read alongside, even as, scripture by the Corinthian church. In fact, some manuscripts have 1 Clement as part of what we call the New Testament. So Clement, the author of this letter was a well-respected Roman presbyter, a successor of Peter.

The legend is that this Clement may have been a slave in the household of Titus Flavius Clemens, a grandson of Vespasian's older brother.

Historically, we know Titus Flavius Clemens was an official during the reign of Domitian, and was consul in 95 CE before being executed that same year by the emperor on the charge of atheism, according to Suetonius. For the Romans, atheism was with respect to the Roman gods. Sometimes Jews were condemned by Roman authorities on charges of atheism, not because the Jewish persons did not believe in Yahweh, but because they did not recognize the Roman deities. The idea that Titus Flavius Clemens was executed on charges of atheism creates a romantic notion that he was a Christian. Moreover, there are Christian catacombs that bear the name of his wife, Flavia Domitilla. So for many, the attraction in naming this powerful husband and wife as Christians is strong. Some even maintain a fanciful opinion of identifying Saint Clement not merely as a slave in the household of Titus Flavius Clemens, but with Titus Flavius Clemens himself! Few if any scholars would accept such an identification. It is more likely that Clement may have been a slave in the household of Titus Flavius Clemens but even that identification is a stretch. There is no solid evidence, only circumstantial—the name of Clement himself. And Clement was certainly a fairly common name in first-century Rome. We will learn more about Titus Flavius Clemens when we see the catacombs named for his wife. For today, we shall keep our focus on Saint Clement, and the little we know of him.

In the New Testament, there is only one mention of a Clement. In his letter to the Philippians, Paul says, "Yes, and I ask you also, my true yokemate, to help them, for they have struggled at my side in promoting the gospel, along with Clement and my other co-workers, whose names are in the book of life" (4:3). Could this Clement of Philippians 4:3 be the Clement of Rome, the author of 1 Clement? Much depends on where Paul was when he wrote Philippians, and whether Philippians is a composite letter, i.e., made up of at least two letters to the Philippians. But like we noted in the paragraph above, the connection is tenuous here too; it's merely a name. There is no way to prove the connection between the Clement in Philippians and the author of 1 Clement.

Irenaeus, writing in his *Against the Heresies*, says this about Clement:

> The blessed apostles, therefore, having founded and built up the Church, handed over to Linus the bishopric for administrating the Church. In his epistle to Timothy, Paul mentions this Linus. Anacletus succeeded him; after him, in third place from the apostles, Clement acquired the bishopric. He both saw the blessed apostles themselves and conferred with them, and still had the preaching of the apostles ringing in his ears and their tradition before his

eyes. In this he was not alone, for there were many others still left at that time who had been taught by the apostles.

It was under this Clement that no small dissension arose among the brethren at Corinth. The Church of Rome wrote a very forceful letter to the Corinthians, [thus] uniting them in peace, renewing their faith, and proclaiming the tradition which it had but recently received from the apostles....

Evaristus succeeded this Clement, and Alexander [succeeded] Evaristus. Xystus was appointed sixth in line from the apostles, and after him Telesphorus, who was also a most glorious witness. After him came Hyginus, then Pius, and after him Anicetus. Soter succeeded Anicetus; and now Eleutherus, the twelfth in line from the apostles, holds the title of the bishopric.[36]

Though Irenaeus links Clement with the apostles, he does not explicitly link him with Paul. In this he is like Tertullian who never mentions Paul but claims that Clement was ordained by Peter.[37] In fact, it was Origen who first explicitly linked the Clement named in Paul's letter to the Philippians with the author of 1 Clement.[38] St. Jerome (347–420) writing in about 390 says that a church in Rome still bears witness to Clement's memory, and that he died in the third year of Trajan (which would be about 100). But Jerome also admits that it is unclear whether Clement was the fourth or second bishop of Rome.[39]

In place of real knowledge about Clement legends grew. The *Golden Legend* says that Clement was born of noble stock (not a slave) and that he consecrated Domitilla, niece of the Emperor Domitian, as a virgin. The fourth-century *Acta* [of Clement], cited by the *Golden Legend* claims that during the reign of the Emperor Trajan (98–117 CE), Clement was taken to the Black Sea, tied to an anchor, and dropped overboard. We pick up the story according to the *Golden Legend*:

> A great crowd stood at the water's edge, and Cornelius and Probus, Clement's disciples, bade all the people pray that the Lord would show them the martyr's body. At once the sea drew back three miles, and all walked out dry-shod and found a small building prepared by God in the shape of a temple, and within, in an ark, the body of Saint Clement and the anchor beside him.

36. Irenaeus, *Against Heresies* 3.3.3 in *Irenaeus: Against the Heresies*, 32–33.
37. Tertullian, *Prescription of the Heretics*, 32.
38. Origen, *Commentary on John*, 36 in PG 14.293–94.
39. Jerome, *On Illustrious Men*, 15 in PL 22.631–34.

It was revealed to Clement's disciples that they were not to remove his body. Every year thereafter, at the date of his passion, the sea receded three miles and stayed back for a week, affording dry passage to those who came. In one of these annual solemnities a woman went out to the shrine with her little son, and the child fell asleep. When the ceremony was finished and the sound of the inrushing tide was heard, the woman was terrified and forgot her son in her hurry to get ashore with the rest of the crowd. Then she remembered, and loud were the cries and lamentations she addressed to heaven, wailing and running up and down the beach, hoping she might see the child's body cast up by the waves. When all hope was gone, she went home and mourned and wept for a whole year. Then, when the sea drew back, she was the first to reach the shrine, running ahead of the crowd to see whether she might find some trace of her son. She prayed devoutly at Saint Clement's tomb, and when she rose from prayer she saw the child asleep where she had left him. Thinking that he must be dead she moved closer, ready to gather up the lifeless body; but when she saw that he was sleeping, she quickly awakened him and, in full sight of the crowd, lifted him in her arms. She asked him where he had been throughout the year, and he said he did now know if a year had passed and though that he had slept soundly for one night.[40]

This legend and the others about Clement in the *Golden Legend*, offer next to nothing by way of historical detail. But do offer tremendous help in deciphering the frescoes on the walls of the fourth-century church.

The *Acta* was so influential that in the ninth century it inspired Cyril and Methodius to venture to the Black Sea to look for the bones of Clement. When found, these remains were translated to San Clemente in Rome. This event is also depicted in a fresco in the fourth-century church, though the frescoes would have been done sometime after the journey of Cyril and Methodius but before the Norman sack of Rome in 1084.

The confessio of the twelfth-century church is said to hold the remains of St. Clement and St. Ignatius of Antioch. Many of the furnishings of the fourth-century basilica have been moved to their present location, including the choir and the candlestick. Even the mosaic in the apse is believed to be a copy from the fourth-century basilica. The fourth-century basilica was filled in sometime after the Norman sack of Rome in 1084 so

---

40. De Voragine and Ryan, *Golden Legend*, 717–18.

that the foundation of the ancient church served as the foundation for the twelfth-century church.

As we move down into the fourth-century basilica we see a number of frescoes as noted above.[41] At the main altar we see the final resting place of Dominican Father Mullooly who began the excavations in the late nineteenth century which revealed the earlier structures.

It is in this fourth-century church that Pope St. Gregory the Great in 591 CE gave his famous homily on Mary Magdalene in which he associated her with the prostitute. This homily set the stage for an understanding (or rather misunderstanding) of Mary Magdalene that still persists among the faithful and in the popular culture today.

> This woman, whom Luke calls a sinner, John names Mary. I believe that she is the same Mary of whom Mark says that seven demons had been cast out. How should we interpret the seven demons except as the totality of vices? ... It is evident, my friends, that a woman who had earlier been eager for actions which are not allowed had used the ointment as a scent for her own body. What she had earlier used disgracefully for herself she now laudably offered for the Lord. Her eyes had sought earthly things; now, chastising them through repentance, she wept. She had used her hair to beautify her face; now she used it to wipe away her tears. She had spoken proudly with her mouth, but in kissing the Lord's feet she fixed it to the footsteps of the Redeemer. She found as many things to sacrifice as she had had ways of offering pleasure. She converted the number of her faults into the number of virtues, so that she could serve God as completely in repentance as she had rejected him in sin.[42]

The medieval *Golden Legend* echoing Gregory, says about Mary Magdalene:

> Mary is called Magdalene, which is understood to mean "remaining guilty," or it means armed, or unconquered, or magnificent. These meanings point to the sort of woman she was before, at the time of, and after her conversion ... Renowned as she was for her beauty and her riches, she was no less known for the way she

---

41. For more on the frescos of this important basilica including the fantastic Clementine legends, see Boyle, *A Short Guide to St. Clement's Rome* and Kane, "The Painted Decoration of the Church of San Clemente" in Boyle et al., *San Clemente Miscellany II*.

42. Gregory I, *Gregory the Great*, 269–70.

gave her body to pleasure—so much so that her proper name was forgotten and she was commonly called, "the sinner."[43]

Students of the New Testament today read the gospels a bit differently than did the ancients or medievals. For one, there are so many Marys in the New Testament that it is not possible to connect all of them as one and the same person. We have Mary the Mother of Jesus, Mary of Magdala (Luke 8:2 et al.), Mary of Bethany (John 11:1—12:8; Luke 10:38–41), Mary, mother of James (Mark 16:1), Mary, the mother of James the younger and of Joses (Mark 15:40), Mary, mother of Joses (Mark 15:47), Mary, wife of Clopas (John 19:25), "the other Mary" (Matt 27:61; 28:1), Mary, mother of John Mark (Acts 12:12), and a Mary named by Paul in Romans 16:6. And these are only the women named Mary! There are also unnamed women in the New Testament, in particular the sinful woman who was pardoned by Jesus (Luke 7:37–39) and whom Gregory the Great and the *Golden Legend* take to be Mary Magdalene. But this story of the unnamed sinful woman is unrelated to Mary Magdalene in Luke.

> Afterward he journeyed from one town and village to another, preaching and proclaiming the good news of the kingdom of God. Accompanying him were the Twelve and some women who had been cured of evil spirits and infirmities, Mary, called Magdalene, from whom seven demons had gone out, Joanna, the wife of Herod's steward Chuza, Susanna, and many others who provided for them out of their resources (Luke 8:1–3).

And though Mary Magdalen had seven demons cast out, that does not make her a sinner. We recall that in the ancient world, diseases or other maladies that were not able to be diagnosed were ascribed to demon possession. In fact, some propose that Mary Magdalene might have even suffered from depression, or some other related issue. Such a state might surely have been diagnosed as "possessed by demons." From whatever Mary Magdalene suffered, there is no evidence in the New Testament to claim she was a sinner. But because of the homily delivered here by Pope Gregory, Mary Magdalene has been in the popular imagination a pardoned prostitute (and thus sinner) ever since.

Back at St. Clemente, we are able to venture down into history several more centuries as we descend another staircase to Roman street level at

---

43. De Voragine and Ryan, *Golden Legend*, 375.

the time of Domitian (81–96 CE). We find at this level that we have in fact crossed the street (or narrow alley). We see now an ancient Mithraeum.

The worship of Mithras, open only to men and with its roots in Persia, became popular in Rome in the second century CE, though it has origins in Rome from about 80 CE.

Mithraism understood that there were two powers in opposition: Ahura-Mazda, the lord of life and light, and Ahriman, lord of death and darkness. Mithras, a god, created by Ahura-Mazda from a rock, was the intermediary between humanity and Ahura-Mazda. Mithras, allied with the sun, fought darkness and death on behalf of humanity.

For its adherents, there were seven levels of initiation that correspond to the seven celestial bodies/gods known in antiquity: Mercury, Venus, Mars, Jupiter, Moon, Sun, and Saturn. Initiation ceremonies were conducted in caves or cave-like dwellings (as we see near the first-century house), for the cave represents the cosmos. The Mithraic myth of creation states that Mithras struggled with the first living creature, the bull. He seized it, dragged it to a cave, but it escaped. The Sun then sent a raven to inform Mithras of the calamity and of his task to find and kill the bull. Mithras did just that, and from the blood of that bull flowed the cosmos.

When we see the Mithraeum, you will be able to see a relief of Mithras slaying the bull depicted on the altar. In this room also notice the long marble "couches" where the ritual meal would be eaten in typical Roman custom, lying on one's side. In the Mithraic antechamber you will see stucco ceilings. Also there is a Mithraic "schoolroom" with paintings. In these rooms, look for scenes from the Mithraic myth outlined above.

Across the narrow alleyway, we come to a first-century domicile. Though there is no direct evidence that Titus Flavius Clemens lived here, the fact that the church was named Saint Clement's leads one to that speculation. Further excavations show that this ground level was in fact built on top of some damaged structures from the great fire of 64 CE.

So we have seen nearly twenty centuries of history, faith, art, legends, myths, and more in our brief visit to this basilica. We have seen the transformation of a Roman house into the foundation of a Christian basilica. That basilica itself, though damaged by war, becomes the foundation for yet another sacred place. This most recent basilica has stood then for more than 800 years. In those centuries the city has continued to grow around it so that now we descend from street level to the portico. The twelfth-century basilica uses furnishings from its fourth-century predecessor while incorporating a (relatively) new confessio (1868).

Santa Pudenziana

We read from the final chapter of the second letter to Timothy, a letter that some have characterized as a "last will and testament" of Paul, at Tre Fontane. We recall the conclusion to the letter here, where the author makes reference to a certain man by the name of "Pudens."

> Greet Prisca and Aquila and the family of Onesiphorus. Erastus remained in Corinth, while I left Trophimus sick at Miletus. Try to get here before winter. Eubulus, Pudens, Linus, Claudia, and all the brothers send greetings. The Lord be with your spirit. Grace be with all of you (2 Tim 4:19–22).

Tradition says that this letter was written by Paul from Rome, though modern scholarly opinion differs. But with only this name, Pudens, a legend developed which grew to include the churches of Santa Pudenziana and Santa Prassede. That is, the Pudens named in 2 Tim 4:21 was the son of Quintus Cornelius Pudens, a Roman senator (known only in the legend. There is no other evidence to indicate Senator Pudens was a historical figure). Senator Pudens and Priscilla, his wife, became Christian converts by Peter, who stayed at their house. The Senator's son, also named Pudens, was baptized by Peter as were his children, Novatus, Timotheus, Pudentiana, and Praxedes, all of whom were remembered as saints. The legend says that Pudens was martyred during the persecution of Nero following the great fire of Rome. The sisters were celebrated in the Roman calendar until their names were removed in the reform of 1969.

There is also fanciful scholarly conjecture about Pudens based on epigrams of Martial (4.13; 11:53), for Aulus Pudens was an Umbrian centurion and friend of Martial. This is no mere legend! So it is tempting for some to associate this Aulus Pudens with that named by Paul. Furthermore, Martial writes that Aulus Pudens married Claudia Peregrina (Claudia, 'the foreigner'), perhaps also known as Claudia Rufina from Britain, also mentioned by Martial. This gives us two of the names mentioned in 2 Tim, both Pudens and Claudia, and so it is a tantalizing suggestion. But the names Pudens and Claudia are separated by Linus in Paul's Second Letter to Timothy, making any marriage between the two and therefore any association with Martial's Pudens unlikely. Even more, the name Claudia was fairly common, and the name Pudens was not uncommon. Still, we see how far many will go in their attempts to connect mere names in Scripture with historical persons of note.

Today, it is possible to visit the churches named for the daughters. When we approach Santa Pudenziana we immediately recognize the church as far below modern street level. But of course this is only because the streets and city of Rome have grown upward with time. We are literally descending into the past with each step we take closer to the entrance of the church.

This church is also significant in that according to legend, it was the residence of the Popes until the time of Constantine, when the Lateran was given to them. Excavations from the twentieth century however revealed the church dating from the last decade of the fourth century. Moreover, the church had been built into pre-existing baths, which casts doubt on the legend that this was the papal residences.

Not much from the early church survived as so many centuries have passed, but the mosaics in the apse draw our attention in part because the apostles (ten rather than twelve) are depicted in Roman senatorial garb. The mosaics were restored in the nineteenth century and are said to be based on the fourth-century design. They are one of the earliest artistic representations in mosaic of Peter and Paul. Interestingly, both are bearded, not clean shaven as would have been the custom for Roman men. And Paul's head of hair is thinning as is his face; whereas Peter's hair is full, like his face. These early likenesses will be seen again and again throughout the city.

We are reminded of the physical description of Paul in the second-century work, The Acts of Paul:

> A man small of stature, with a bald head and crooked legs, in a good state of body, with eyebrows meeting and nose somewhat hooked, full of friendliness; for now he appeared like a man, and now he had the face of an angel.[44]

Upon leaving this church we might walk over to Santa Prassede, the church named after Pudenziana's legendary sister.

Santa Prassede

For the legend of Santa Prassede, see the material for church named after her sister, Santa Pudenziana.

44. Acts of Paul and Thecla 2. *NTA* 2.239.

There had been a church bearing the name Praxede from the late fifth century. But the church we visit was built by Pope Paschal I (817–824). One of the most interesting aspects of this particular church is the chapel of St. Zeno on the right hand side, which has beautiful and significant mosaics. One in particular has attracted attention more recently. There is an image of a woman with a square nimbus, which indicates that she is still alive (a round nimbus indicates that the person is deceased). The words to the left read "Theodora" and above, "Episcopa" which would ordinarily be translated as "bishop." But many guidebooks, including the one published by this church, will say that Theodora was the mother of Pope Paschal I, and this (episcopa) was a title for the papal mother. Interestingly, we do not hear of many (or really any) other mothers of popes being called "episcopa." The meaning one discerns from this mosaic likely depends on one's presuppositions regarding issues of women and ordination.

In the confessio of this church we will find the purported remains of the sisters Pudenziana and Prassede, along with a sponge said to have been used to wipe up the blood of the martyrs.

5

Pauline Sites Outside the Walls; Appia Antica

Abbey of the Three Fountains
(Abbazia delle Tre Fontane)

WHEN WE VISIT THIS site we will see three churches: Ss. Vincenzo e Anastasio (The Medieval Cistercian Abbey Church, today of the Trappists), Santa Maria Scala Coeli (the Church of Our Lady Stairway to Heaven), and San Paolo alle Tre Fontane (Saint Paul at Three Fountains) the church of the martyrdom of St. Paul.

As to the legendary place of Paul's martyrdom, we learned in the introductory material about the Acts of Paul, and the Acts of Peter and Paul, that the accounts grew in their passing on detail. Some of the earlier accounts, including the Acts of Paul (59)[1] and the *Passio* (59), and even the *Liber Pontificalis* (22), place Paul's death on the via Ostiense. The later sixth-century work, the Greek version of the *Acts of Peter and Paul* (80), introduces a new location, or specifies the location, as the Aquae Salviae, heretofore never mentioned in the traditional and legendary material about Paul's death, as we reviewed on page 19.

> The sentence having been handed down, Peter and Paul were removed from Nero's presence. Paul was led, chained, to the place where he was to be decapitated, three miles from the City, by an escort of three soldiers of noble blood.
>
> When they were about an arrow's flight from the city gate, there came to them a pious woman who, when she saw Paul in chains, was greatly moved and burst into tears. The woman's name was Perpetua and she had only one eye. Seeing her weeping, Paul said to her: "Give me your scarf and at my return I shall give it back to you." She took her scarf and immediately gave it to him. The soldiers approached the woman and said to her: "Woman, why do you wish to lose your scarf? Do you not know that he is on his way to be decapitated?" But Perpetua answered them: "I beseech you, by Caesar's sword, to cover his eyes with this scarf when you behead him." And so it was.
>
> They beheaded him at the demesne of the Aquae Salviae (*eis massan kaloumenēn Akouai Salbias*), near the pine-tree. According to God's will, before the soldiers returned, the scarf, soaked with blood, was restituted to the woman and as soon as she put it on, her eye was suddenly opened.[2]

Thus is the name "Aquae Salviae" mentioned, giving us the legendary source for this site, as it was known in antiquity. It would have been named for the family of Salvius, a prominent second-century-CE family who most likely owned this property as part of their estates. In a still later legend (sixth–seventh-century work, Historiae Apostolicae of Pseudo-Abdias), after Paul's martyrdom at the Salvian waters, one of his disciples, Lucina,

---

1. The Passio chapter 59, as the Acts of Paul chapter 59, state simply that that "Paul was decapitated on the Ostian Road" (Eastman, *Ancient Martyrdom Accounts*, 265).

2. From Tajra, *Martyrdom of St. Paul*, 148–49. For another modern translation, see Eastman, *Ancient Martyrdom Accounts*, 307.

moved his body to a proper burial site which her family owned near the Ostiense (present day Saint Paul Outside the Walls).

The question becomes, why did the later legend develop, placing Paul's martyrdom not at the Ostiense as earlier sources had it, but at the Salvian Waters? And why did this legend develop so late? Tajra has an interesting hypothesis. He notes that Benedict of Soracte (c. 1000 CE) ascribed the foundation of a Church and a Monastery at the Salvian Waters to a Byzantine general by the name of Narses, who ruled Rome from 548–67 CE. Of course, Benedict of Soracte is a late source for this detail so his work is used with caution. Prior to this being known as a church of Saint Paul, it was referred to in the seventh century as the Cilician Monastery at the Salvian Waters. As the monks were Cilician, they would have been open to their monastery being linked with Paul, for whom being a Cilician was something in common (Acts 9:11; 21:39; 22:3). Thus, these Cilician monks were likely the source and the reason for the place of Paul's martyrdom being shifted from the Ostiense to the Salvian Waters where their monastery stood. As Tajra concludes:

> The story associating the Acquae Salviae site with Paul's death is completely unhistorical. It was a legend elaborated by the resident Cilician monks, who particularly venerated Paul, to confer greater glory and renown on their new monastic foundation by linking the site on which it was buil[t] to Paul's martyrdom.[3]

On this matter, Eastman disputes Tajra. He sees three important pieces of evidence pointing to some historical reliability for the Salvian legend in the Greek Acts. The first is the story of the woman (Perpetua or Lucina) which for Eastman has a Roman provenance. The second and third are tied to the terms for "estate" and "Salvian Waters" which in the Greek text are transliterated Latin terms, *"massa"* and *"Akouai Salbias."* Eastman wonders why Cilician (Greek) monks would invent a tale using Latin terms while writing in Greek. Instead, "the editors of the Greek text must have learned the name of the site from a Roman source, and they took this directly into Greek."[4]

But what of the "Three Fountains"? Tre Fontane (three fountains) gets its name from another, even later legend that when Paul was decapitated his head bounced three times and three fountains sprang forth. The story is

---

3. Tajra, *Martyrdom of St. Paul*, 154.
4. Eastman, *Paul the Martyr*, 65.

found in the fourteenth-century work, *Mirabiliana*: "There was the blessed Paul beheaded; and when he was beheaded, he cried thrice: Jesus, Jesus, Jesus; and in each place a well flowed, after the three leaps of the head."[5]

So as we come to this site, we can recognize how important were the Pauline stories and legends to the early Christians. They were so important that some legends were developed or at least written relatively late and used to support the legitimacy of particular monasteries or sites.

As the name Salvian Waters suggests, the area was known for its water, or in reality, its swampy marshes. For most of the Christian era the area was known for malaria (*mal aria*: literally, bad air). The marshes were notorious mosquito breeding grounds, and as a result, not much was built up here. There were long periods where the site fell into disrepair. Not until the nineteenth century, when the Trappists were given the monastery, did the area become more habitable. The Trappists imported eucalyptus from Australia which thrived in the marshy environment, and helped to manage and even reduce the swampy areas.

It is interesting to note that Thomas Merton (1915–1968) visited this site ca. 1933. He describes his short time here in the *Seven Storey Mountain*.

> But the last week or ten days that I was in Rome were very happy and full of joy, and on one of those afternoons I took the trolley out to San Paolo, and after that got on a small rickety bus which went up a country road into a shallow saucer of a valley in the low hills south of the Tiber, to the Trappist monastery of Tre Fontane. I went in to the dark, austere old church, and liked it. But I was scared to visit the monastery. I thought the monks were too busy sitting in their graves beating themselves with disciplines. So I walked up and down in the silent afternoon, under the eucalyptus trees, and the thought grew on me: "I should like to become a Trappist monk."
>
> There was very little danger of my doing so, then. The thought was only a daydream—and I suppose it is a dream that comes to many men, even men who don't believe in anything. Is there any man who has ever gone through a whole life time without dressing himself up, in his fancy, in the habit of a monk and enclosing himself in a cell where he sits magnificent in heroic austerity and solitude, while all the young ladies who hitherto were cool to his

---

5. Nichols, *Mirabilia Urbis Romae*, 134. Though the Mirabilia is dated to the twelfth century, the legend cited above is from a different (fourteenth-century) manuscript included in the supplementary material of the 1889 English edition.

affections in the world come and beat on the gates of the monastery crying, "Come out, come out!"

Ultimately, I suppose, that is what my dream that day amounted to. I had no idea what Trappist monks were, or what they did, except that they kept silence. In fact, I also thought they lived in cells like the Carthusians, all alone.[6]

As we, like Thomas Merton before us, enter the grounds we see the gate of Charlemagne. We recall that he was crowned emperor in the basilica of St. Peter on Christmas eve in 800 by Pope St. Leo III. And during that time he stayed here. The arched gateway is said to have been a gift from the emperor. We might notice a fairly recent inscription on the side of the gate which reads:

J. Sonnino–A.S.A. Di Porto
Persecutionem Nazistam
In Judaeos dire Saevientem fugientes
hic deipara favente sospites
Beneficii memores
Posuere
A.D. MCMXLIV

translated:
In the year 1944
J. Sonnino and A.S.A. Di Porto
Placed [this inscription] mindful of the blessing
[that] in this place, by the favor of the mother-of-God,
Those fleeing the Nazi Persecution direly raging the Jews found safety

So, as the inscription makes clear, this place was a sanctuary for Jews and others during the Nazi occupation of Rome. Such an inscription makes clear to us that for all their ancient and medieval significance, the churches of Rome continue to play a noteworthy role. Through the gate, we see the Abbey Church on the left and the Stairs of Heaven church on the right.

The Stairs of Heaven is so named because it was in the crypt that the Cistercian reformer St. Bernard of Clairvaux (1090–1153) had a vision of souls ascending a ladder from purgatory into heaven. At this church also are commemorated Saint Zeno and 10,203 soldiers who were martyred here in 299 by the emperor Diocletian. The relics from these martyrs were moved to Santa Prassede in the ninth century. This church's crypt is also noteworthy as another legend states that Paul was held here immediately

---

6. Merton, *The Seven Storey Mountain*, 124–25.

prior to his execution, as signs inform the modern pilgrim of that location. So it is at this site, in the crypt, that we will read the final verses from the last chapter of 2 Timothy, a kind of last will and testament from Paul.

> For I am already being poured out like a libation, and the time of my departure is at hand. I have competed well; I have finished the race; I have kept the faith. From now on the crown of righteousness awaits me, which the Lord, the just judge, will award to me on that day, and not only to me, but to all who have longed for his appearance.
>
> Try to join me soon, for Demas, enamored of the present world, deserted me and went to Thessalonica, Crescens to Galatia, and Titus to Dalmatia. Luke is the only one with me. Get Mark and bring him with you, for he is helpful to me in the ministry. I have sent Tychicus to Ephesus. When you come, bring the cloak I left with Carpus in Troas, the papyrus rolls, and especially the parchments. Alexander the coppersmith did me a great deal of harm; the Lord will repay him according to his deeds. You too be on guard against him, for he has strongly resisted our preaching.
>
> At my first defense no one appeared on my behalf, but everyone deserted me. May it not be held against them! But the Lord stood by me and gave me strength, so that through me the proclamation might be completed and all the Gentiles might hear it. And I was rescued from the lion's mouth. The Lord will rescue me from every evil threat and will bring me safe to his heavenly kingdom. To him be glory forever and ever. Amen.
>
> Greet Prisca and Aquila and the family of Onesiphorus. Erastus remained in Corinth, while I left Trophimus sick at Miletus. Try to get here before winter. Eubulus, Pudens, Linus, Claudia, and all the brothers send greetings. The Lord be with your spirit. Grace be with all of you (2 Tim 4:6–22).

It's not difficult with such words to imagine Paul alone, at the twilight of his life, being held in a Roman prison. We then walk down the pathway to St. Paul at the Three Fountains, the legendary site of his martyrdom. The walk is in silence, as monitory signs indicate. This time can be reflective in the midst of so many site-seeing activities. We ponder Paul's life and the ultimate price he paid for his convictions.

In the church we see mosaic floors from Ostia, commemorating the four seasons. As they were from Ostia, these were (are) pagan rather than Christian. They were installed in this church as a way to preserve them and share their beauty with pilgrims. In the far right corner of the church is displayed the column of Paul's beheading. We also see three altars, each built over one of the fountains, which are now covered. Here perhaps we see testament to one of the more fantastical Roman legends, and it comes from the fourteenth-century *Mirabiliana* (1.5) cited above. According to it, when the soldier struck the head of Paul it bounced three times on the ground as Paul cried, "Jesus, Jesus, Jesus." At each point where Paul's head bounced a fountain sprang forth, thus the name, Three Fountains.

Before we depart this place it's good to stop in the Trappist shop where they sell their famous chocolates and liquors. This faraway place from the hustle and bustle of the city bursts with historical and legendary significance, but in quiet, humble, and rather peaceful way. Many have said it is their favorite site for this reason.

St. Paul Outside the Walls
(San Paolo fuori le mura)

We now visit another of the four major basilicas: St. Peter, St. Mary Major, St. Paul Outside the Walls, and St. John Lateran. This is the site where legend says Paul's disciple, Lucina, brought his body to be buried on the Via Ostiense, the road leading to Ostia, port city of Ancient Rome. A rather small basilica structure was built during the time of Constantine and consecrated on November 18, 324. Shortly thereafter, to accommodate the large number of pilgrims, the basilica was enlarged in part by being rotated

180 degrees on its axis. This shifting of its axis meant there was more room to build a much larger basilica. The diagram from Lanciani[7] shows this quite clearly:

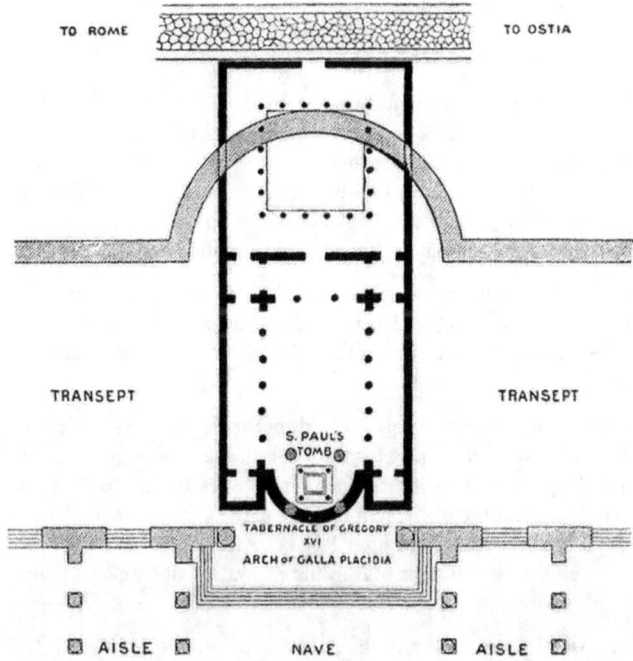

The basilica continued to be enlarged and decorated through the centuries until the terrible night of July 15, 1823. Repairmen on the roof accidentally started a fire which consumed most of the basilica. Thus began a worldwide effort to reconstruct the Basilica of St. Paul Outside the Walls. This is what we have today, a thoroughly reconstructed basilica.

There have been a number of news conferences in recent years surrounding the "discovery" of the tomb of St. Paul. The archeologist overseeing the project, Giorgio Filippi, removed the sarcophagus from its nineteenth-century concrete encasing in Nov–Dec 2006.[8] Since that time

---

7. Diagram from Lanciani, *Pagan and Christian Rome*, 150. Image in Public Domain. Digital image from: https://goo.gl/images/oUoaHw.

8. Tomb of St. Paul to be visible for pilgrims. Catholic News Agency: Rome, Dec 12, 2006 / 12:00 am

> One side of a Roman tomb, long revered as that of St. Paul, has been freed from a 19th-century block of concrete and, thanks to a transparent floor, will soon be visible to the public.

there has been a transparent floor installed near the confessio so that

> Offering a press conference at the Vatican yesterday the Archpriest of St. Paul's Outside-the-Walls, Cardinal Andrea Cordero Lanza di Montezemolo, archeologist, Giorgio Filippi, and basilica official, Pier Carlo Visconti, revealed the results of an ongoing archeological undertaking at the famous basilica.
>
> Filippi said that archeological investigations which have taken place over the last four years uncovered the apse of the original basilica built by the Emperor Constantine in the early part of the fourth century. "On the floor of this building, under the papal altar," he said, "we found that great sarcophagus of which all trace had been lost, considered since the time of Theodosius to be the tomb of St. Paul."
>
> Prior to the discovery, Filippi noted, "although it is an incontrovertible historical fact that the basilica of St. Paul was built over the tomb of the Apostle, the location of the original tomb remained an open question."
>
> According to the archeologist, records of the Benedictine Monastery which is tasked with caring for the basilica, speak of "a great marble sarcophagus found during reconstruction work on the basilica following the great fire of 1823, in the area of the Confession, under the two stones with the inscription PAULO APOSTOLO MART[YRI]. However, there is no trace of it in the excavation documents, unlike the other sarcophagi unearthed on that occasion."
>
> Cardinal Montezemolo told the Italian news service ANSA that the next stage in the work will be to open the tomb, if the Vatican approves. However, he added, "future research will not have to prove that this is Paul's burial place, because there has been agreement on this for 2,000 years."
>
> Filippi, said that while he has "no doubt" the tomb was St Paul's, he was somewhat cautious on what archaeologists might find inside the tomb, saying "it could contain anything".
>
> According to Filippi, the tomb might even be a cenotaph (empty tomb), erected in the name of the saint and "assuming the same value of the tomb itself" - while not actually containing Paul's body, ANSA reported.
>
> "It has a hole on top through which pieces of cloth could be pushed, touching the relic and becoming holy in their turn," Filippi said.
>
> In his talk, Cardinal Montezemolo layed out a plan to completely reorganize the basilica, part of which involves the creation of walking route for pilgrims and visitors including, among other things, a new museum area centered on the monastery's cloister.
>
> The cardinal also spoke extensively of the work taking place around the tomb of St. Paul and mentioned a new transparent floor which

pilgrims may catch a glimpse of the archaeological remains. Many however may be a bit disappointed that the sarcophagus is not clearly indicated, and some struggle to comprehend what they are really seeing through the transparent floor. One thing that is clear is the apse from the original basilica. In any case, the museum, bookstore, and many other improvements imagined in 2006 have now been realized.

As we approach, we can see that the size and scope of the portico is grander than what a fourth-century basilica would have had. Here we experience the purpose of the portico. We are being drawn into sacred space. The noise from the outside is still heard, but it is softer. In the portico we sense geometrical stability, and proportion.

Our eyes are drawn upward to the façade which has been decorated with mosaics depicting four Old Testament prophets: Isaiah, Jeremiah, Ezekiel and Daniel. The four rivers surrounding the lamb represent the four gospels. And we easily recognize the twelve lambs as representing the twelve apostles.

St. Paul Outside the Walls has three main doors. The two most important are the Bronze Door (center, placed there in 1931) and the Jubilee door (on the right, also used as the holy door, placed there in the year 2000).

The center door, also known as the Bronze Door, depicts New Testament scenes in the lives of Peter and Paul, and each door "concludes" with a post-New Testament depiction of their respective martyrdoms, beginning from the bottom and reading up. Peter is on the left; Paul on the right. Reading from the left panels and starting from the bottom we see Peter baptizing in the catacombs; the founding of the Roman see; Giving of the Keys to Peter; Domine, quo vadis; and the crucifixion of Peter. On the right hand, reading from the bottom up we see Paul arriving in Rome, Paul preaching in Rome; Paul's call; Conversion of the centurion; and Paul's beheading with Plautilla holding the scarf, as mentioned in the Passio legend from fourth–fifth century.

---

will make it possible to see the remains of the basilica's Constantinian apse and the tomb.

Montezemolo said that, if tests are approved, they will probably also examine the stone the sarcophagus is made of. St Paul's Outside the Walls, which is about three kilometers outside the ancient walls of Rome is the city's largest church after St Peter's.

http://www.catholicnewsagency.com/new.php?n=8262

The center door at St. Paul Outside the Walls

Entering the basilica we perceive the sacred. The place, though built in the nineteenth century as noted above, gives us a sense of an ancient basilica with its size and proportion. The height of the central nave is twice the height of the side aisle. Light enters from the second story windows. It is quiet here. As we have noticed in other basilicas, there are no pews. Ancient worshipers would have been standing throughout the service, which would have lasted longer than 60 minutes.

Near the second story windows we see in medallions, mosaics of the popes back to Peter. Near the main altar of the church, on the right, we see the portraits of John Paul II, Benedict XVI, and now Pope Francis.

The altar with its canopy has in its confessio the relics of St. Paul himself. On a marble slab is a famous inscription, dating from about the fourth or fifth century CE, PAULO APOSTOLO MART . . . There the marble slab is broken. Even so, the translation is "to Paul, Apostle [and] Martyr." This is a much more precise and clean indication of Paul's remains than the "graffiti wall" we see at St. Peter's. The slab has three holes in it. The circular hole was used to burn incense. The other holes were made after the inscription. They are thought to have been used by the faithful who would lower pieces of cloth or other articles to touch the remains of St. Paul. The marble slab may now be seen in the Basilica's museum.

Elements around the altar that survive from the earlier basilica include the candlestick from the twelfth century, and the canopy by Arnolfo di Cambio (ca. 1245–1310) from the thirteenth century. The mosaic in the apse is a copy of the tenth-century original that was destroyed in the fire. The chapel of the Blessed Sacrament is worthy of note. It has a wooden crucifix whose head is said to have turned toward the mystic and visionary St. Bridget of Sweden (1303–1373) when she prayed here in 1350. She was in Rome for a Jubilee Year (during the Avignon Papacy). Her devotion to the passion of Jesus led her to want to know exactly how many blows Jesus received during his ordeal. She is said to have received the answer from him here: 5480. She also received fifteen prayers to recite in honor of these wounds. Her visions and prayers were extremely popular in the late Middle Ages, when devotion to Christ's passion was particularly strong. This chapel is also where Ignatius and his companions made their vows as Jesuits on April 22, 1541. Through the Oratory of St. Julian we walk to the thirteenth-century cloister, with columns decorated in Cosmatesque style.

A rose garden beautifies the cloister of St. Paul Outside the Walls, and various inscriptions found in the vicinity decorate the walls. Beyond the cloister on the left we will find the chapel of relics.

As we prepare to depart it might seem that the place is not quite fitting for Saint Paul, the purported author of nearly a quarter of the New Testament. It's been said that the basilica and its environs have all the charm of a train station. Perhaps there is some truth in that. The basilica lacks the majesty and beauty of St. Peter's. It is large, shiny, and new, almost stripped of its earlier character. Even though it is built according to proper proportions, it seems to lack a soul, and possibly resembles a museum more than a basilica. But sitting under the portico listening to the tour busses waiting for their clients we ponder the meaning of the Apostle to the Gentiles.

As comfortable speaking Greek as Hebrew and citing Moses as the Greek poets. Paul was a man who has been called the "true" founder of Christianity, for he brought the Gospel to the Gentiles and they quickly became the dominant force in this early movement. So in that way it may be appropriate that the basilica that bears his name is on the Ostiense, the road leading from Rome to Ostia. Paul, a religious minority who enjoyed the citizenship of Rome, was beheaded outside the walls, which is where we find ourselves.

Ancient Appian Way
(Appia Antica)

The Appian Way, a road from Rome to Capua (near modern Naples) was initially constructed in 312 BCE by the Censor Appius Claudius Caecus.[9] Over the centuries it was extended until finally it reached Brindisium on the Adriatic coast of Italy. The Appian Way leads out of Rome, through the Alban hills, to the Pontine Marshes of the plains. These marshes as the name would suggest were swampy and made for miserable, smelly travel. Eventually, canals were made to run alongside that section of the Appian Way.

9. Appius Claudius Caecus also built the first aqueduct in Rome, the Aqua Appia in 312 BCE which was about 16 km long, entering the city at what became the Porta Maggiore.

The Appian Way is historically significant in so many ways. Statius (c. 45–96 CE) in his *Silvae* (2.2) calls it the "Regina viarum," the "queen of the roads." The slave rebellion led by Spartacus was put to a vicious end when the captured slaves were crucified along the Appian Way in 70 BCE. The crosses went from Rome to Capua as nearly 6000 slaves were crucified following the rebellion (Appian, *Civil Wars*, 1.120). The Appian Way carried soldiers and goods throughout the republican and imperial era of Rome. According to Acts of the Apostles, Paul would have traveled it from Puteoli to Rome; and according to legend Peter fled the city by means of it. Along its way were villas, cemeteries, catacombs, circuses, taverns, and almost anything else you could expect to find. In the eighteenth century a new Appia (Via Appia Nuova) was built near the old. Its historical significance continues to the present day.

Near the place of the Domitilla catacombs we can see the Mausoleo delle Fosse Ardeatine which is a memorial to one of the most horrendous acts on Italian soil during WWII. On March 23, 1944 the Italian resistance killed thirty-two German soldiers. The following day the Nazis killed 335 people in revenge, including Jews, priests, civilians, and even a fourteen-year-old boy at this site, the Fosse Ardeatine. Those arrested by the Nazis were simply shot, execution style in the back of the head, while kneeling in the caves. After the executions, explosives were used to collapse the caves over the corpses. In early June, 1944 Allied tanks and troops rolled down the Appian Way and liberated Rome from the Nazis on June 4, only two days before D-Day. The 335 who were killed by the Nazis were later exhumed and given a proper burial.

Today, we walk a portion of the Appian Way and we tie our personal story to the story of this ancient way. Literally millions of people have walked these stones for centuries. The stones have borne the feet of those who bring good news. The stones have also borne the feet of soldiers, some to conquer, others to liberate. Now these same stones bear our feet.

Domine Quo Vadis?
(Lord, where are you going?)

Along the Ancient Appian Way not far outside the ancient city we find this rather plain church, built at a fork in the road where legend has it that Jesus appeared to Peter. We recall this sixth-century legend from the Latin version of the Acts of Peter, referred to as Pseudo-Linus *Martyrdom of Blessed*

Peter the Apostle. The Latin work is attributed to Linus, the bishop of Rome, but that authorship is spurious, thus the "Pseudo-Linus." This Latin version of the story gives us the "Domine, quo vadis" story. In it, Peter flees the city of Rome only to meet Jesus, who is going to Rome. Peter asks Jesus, "Lord, where are you going?" (Domine, quo vadis?) to which Jesus replies, "I am going to Rome to be crucified again."[10]

As we step into this church we can see an odd-looking replica of the stone that is said to bear the footprints of Jesus from this encounter. The "original" stone with the "actual footprints" of Jesus is at S. Sebastiano.

If we proceed along the Appia Antica a bit further we will come across another fork in the road, at Vicolo della Caffarella. Assassins sent by King Henry VIII (1491–1547) had been sent to kill Cardinal Pole in 1539. The Cardinal was in exile in Rome after he sparred with King Henry when the latter rejected the authority of the Pope. When the Cardinal escaped the assassins' plot he erected this chapel, where it came to mark another possible location of St. Peter's encounter with the Risen Lord.[11]

Domitilla Catacombs

Along the Appian Way we come across the Domitilla Catacombs. It was Roman law that cemeteries were to be outside the city. These tombs as well as those on the scavi tour at St. Peter's were outside the ancient city of Rome. As opposed to the funerary monuments or mausoleums we saw beneath St. Peter's on the scavi tour, catacombs were generally for poorer people who could not afford large monuments to their deceased loved ones. Instead, a small piece of property could be excavated for the deposition of corpses. Think of the catacombs as an underground apartment complex for the deceased, rather than a sprawling cemetery on the surface. The volcanic soil known as tufa made for excellent underground chambers as it is easy to pick, but extremely stable and strong under pressure. The marshy soil around Chicago for example could not support such excavations. But here in and around Rome, excavations could continue deeper and deeper into the ground.

Christians have been visiting the catacombs for centuries. Even St. Jerome gives us an account of his visits as a young man:

---

10. Pseudo-Linus, *Martyrdom of Blessed Peter the Apostle* in Eastman *Ancient Martyrdom Accounts*, 42.

11. Masson, *Companion Guide to Rome*, 458.

When I was studying the liberal arts in Rome as a youth, on the Lord's days I used to go around with others of the same age and intention to the tombs of the apostles and martyrs. And frequently I entered the crypts that had been hollowed out of the deep places of the earth and that, along the walls on either side of those who enter, hold the bodies of the people buried there. Everything is dark, almost to the point of fulfilling the words of the prophet: "Let them go down to hell alive" [Ps 55:15]. Seldom is light let in from above to relieve the horror of darkness, so that you should think not so much of light let in through a window as through a keyhole. And then, as one proceeds step-by-step, you are surrounded by blind night and the following line of Virgil suggests itself: "On all sides my spirit is in dread, and the very silence is terrifying."[12]

Thankfully, the modern world has electricity, so when we visit the catacombs we have the benefit of light, and are not reliant upon natural light seldom let in "through a keyhole." This visit will be anything but terrifying!

The Domitilla catacombs burst with history, martyrology, legend, and a sense of the sacred. They are so named after Flavia Domitilla, who owned the land, according to legend and confirmed by archeological findings. For example, when we enter the basilica, look on the right-hand side wall between the two sarcophagi to see her name inscribed on a funeral monument, found near this location.[13]

---

12. Jerome, *On Ezekiel* (12.40), in *St. Jerome*, 451.

13. This inscription (CIL 6.8942) has been reconstructed in various ways by different scholars. For our purposes, it is sufficient to note Flavia Domitilla's name clearly on line 4. A particularly helpful discussion is found in Cook, *Roman Attitudes Toward the Christians*, 128–30.

TATIA·BAVCYL[...
TRIX·SEPIEM·LIB[...
DIVI·VESPASIAN[...
FLAVIAE·DOMITIL[...
VESPASIANI·NEPTIS·A[...
IUS·BENEFICIO·HOC·SEPHULCRV[...
MEIS·LIBERTIS·LIBERTABVS·PO[...

As we reviewed in the material about San Clemente (pages 99–100), historically, Flavia was the granddaughter of the emperor Vespasian, conqueror of Jerusalem. The emperor Domitian was her uncle. She was married to Titus Flavius Clemens, who was a great nephew of Vespasian and brother of Titus Flavius Sabinus. Domitian seems to have taken an interest in Clemens' two sons, renaming them T. Flavius Vespasianus and T. Flavius Domitianus, appointing them his successor, and procuring Quintilian (ca. 35 CE–ca. 100 CE) the master rhetorician as their tutor.[14] Titus Flavius Clemens

---

14. Quintilian, *Institutes of Oratory*, IV, Proemium 2.

himself served as consul together with the emperor Domitian in 95 CE. But from there things turned sour quickly. According to the Roman historian Suetonius, in that year Domitian condemned Titus Flavius Clemens to death on "a very slight suspicion."[15]

Another ancient historian, but writing a century later than Suetonius, is Cassius Dio, who tells us that both Titus Flavius Clemens and his wife Domitilla were charged with atheism, "a charge on which many others who drifted into Jewish ways were condemned. Some of these were put to death, and the rest were at least deprived of their property. Domitilla was merely banished to Pandateria."[16] Atheism in this context was with respect to the Roman gods.

At least one modern scholar puts forth the notion that Titus Flavius Clemens, being the sole surviving member of the Flavian house, could have been a thorn in the side of Domitian. "The fact that Domitian had adopted Clemens' two young sons, renaming them T. Flavius Vespasianus and T. Flavius Domitianus and clearly marking them out as his successors, may have given Clemens and his wife Domitilla delusions of grandeur, affecting their behavior in a way intolerable to Domitian."[17]

Though Domitian had Clemens executed in 95, he lasted about only another year in power himself, as he was assassinated by a steward of Flavia Domitilla named Stephanus, who also had help from some others.[18]

A sketch of the family tree of Flavia Domitilla and her husband Titus Flavius Clemens:

---

15. Suetonius, *Domitian*, 15, in *Lives of the Caesars*. He also tells us in the same paragraph that Clemens was extremely lazy.
16. Cassius Dio, "Epitome of Book LXVII," in *Roman History*, 67.14.2b–3a.
17. Southern, *Domitian*, 116.
18. Cf. Suetonius, *Domitian*, 17, in *Lives of the Caesars*.

Vespasian[19] ===[married to]=== (Flavia) Domitilla the Elder
‖
‖
(Flavia) Domitilla the younger ==[married to]=== (unknown husband)
(the only daughter of Vespasian)[20]
‖
‖
Flavia Domitilla ===[married to]===Titus Flavius Clemens
(son of Sabinus III)[21]
‖
‖
2 sons (renamed by Domitian and made heirs) and five other children[22]

No ancient Roman author says that Flavia or Clemens were condemned for being Christian. However, the legend quickly grew (e.g., Acts of Nereus and Achilleus), and produced speculation that a slave or other member of the household of Titus Flavius Clemens would have been the Clement of Rome who penned 1 Clement, and who is known as the fourth bishop of Rome. For more on that, see the section in this book on the Church of Saint Clement. And much later legends have Flavia Domitilla professing virginity and giving Saint Clement a sign of that profession. As mentioned above in Part I of the book, much of the stories read as "fan fiction" and have little or no basis in historical fact.

The catacombs that bear the name Domitilla were so named because in antiquity this land was the cemetery of the Flavians (Domitilla's family). Besides the remains of her family, the catacombs also contain the relics of hundreds of early Christians. Moreover, they hold some of the most treasured Christian works of art from the second century including the paintings of Daniel in the Lion's Den and the earliest known representation of Jesus the Good Shepherd.

---

19. Born 9 CE; married 38 CE; reigned 69–79 CE.

20. Vespasian and Flavia Domitilla the Elder had three adult children: Flavia Domitilla the younger, Titus (r. 79–81 CE), and Domitian (r. 81–96 CE).

21. Sabinus III was the son of Flavius Sabinus, who was the older brother of Vespasian.

22. It is clear from the inscription cited above (CIL 6.8942) that Titus Flavius Clemens and Flavia Domitilla had a total of seven children, though it seems likely that as many as five died as infants as we learn only of the two sons, renamed, as adults.

The tour begins after paying the fee, by descending a staircase to a contemporary lower level, which would have been ground level in antiquity. We enter into the foyer of the Ancient Basilica of Nereus and Achilleus. There is an inscription from Pope Damasus (366–384) about Nereus and Achilleus, an image of which is reproduced here:

Damasus composed this as a poem in imitation of Virgil's hexameter style. As one can see in the image, only the lower left and right hand corners are original. The text has been reconstructed based on medieval manuscripts. The reconstruction (with spaces added between Latin words) and translation are as follows:

NEREUS ET ACHILLEVS MARTYRES
MILITIAE NOMEN DEDERANT SAEVUMQ[UE] GEREBANT
OFFICIUM PARITER SPECTANTES IUSSA TYRANNI
PRAECEPTIS PULSANTE METU SERVIRE PARATI
MIRA FIDES RERUM SUBITO POSUERE FUROREM
CONVERSI FUGIUNT DUCIS IMPIA CASTRA RELINQUUNT
PROICIUNT CLIPEOS FALERAS TELAQ[UE] CRUENTA
CONFESSI GAUDENT CHRISTI PORTARE TRIUMFOS
CREDITE PER DAMASUM POSSIT QUID GLORIA CHRISTI

> Nereus and Achilleus Martyrs
> They had enrolled in the army and they waged a savage office
> Obeying equally the orders of a tyrant,
> Being prepared to serve [his] orders under great fear.
> Faith the wonder of things: Suddenly they put down their rage
> Converted they flee, relinquish the wicked camp of their leader,
> Cast down their shields, military armaments, and bloody spears
> Having confessed they are rejoicing to carry the triumphs of Christ.
> Believe through Damasus what the glory of Christ can do.

The legend of Nereus and Achilleus is attested to in many ancient texts, including this inscription above. But there is little agreement as to the historical character of these legends. Basically, the two soldiers who served in the early fourth century were said to have converted to Christianity, given up their military careers, and then faced martyrdom. Based on this skeletal story many fantastical details were added, including most significantly retrojecting their service to coincide with Flavia Domitilla, so that they were in effect her bodyguards! In that role they gave many speeches about the advantages of virginity, and saw to it that Flavia remained a virgin to the point that she professed that to Saint Clement. It seems that their remains and those of Flavia's were thought to be in this catacomb structure, therefore uniting the Christians not only in geography but in legend. Eventually in the ninth century, their remains, along with Flavia Domitilla's were brought to the church of Nereus and Achilleus closer to the city, which is also known as the church of the bandage (see section in this book on the Mamertine prison).

Three Taverns
(Tre Taverne)

Tre Taverne or "Three Taverns" seems to have been a kind of "whistle stop café" to borrow a term from Garrison Keillor. Though modern scholars are unsure of the precise location of this ancient way stop, the term tavern (*taberna*) in Latin could mean anything from an inn with overnight accommodations to a booth more akin to a modern kiosk. Most likely, Three Taverns was a place where travelers might get supplies, water, bread, or other sustenance. There survive letters that Cicero wrote from the place, in one of which he describes meeting a slave there whom Atticus, Cicero's dear friend, had sent with news for Cicero. Cicero dashes off a letter at four in the afternoon (Letter 36, to Atticus). Six hours later he sent another letter to Atticus, this time from Forum Appius (Letter 37, to Atticus). In Letter 39 Cicero laments that Atticus never received the letter he wrote and dispatched from Three Taverns (i.e., Letter 36).

From these and other letters the ancient world comes alive. The ancient letter is a familiar genre not only to those who study the New Testament. What was it like to live in a world when communication was not instantaneous? By necessity, Cicero depended on travelers headed back to Rome to carry his letters. Atticus in turn sends a slave with a message for Cicero. Though Cicero is only a day's journey from Rome, he is completely dependent on others for communication.

Not only was Three Taverns a stop mentioned in Classical literature, but Luke mentions it too, in his last chapter of Acts: "In two days we reached Puteoli [modern day Puzzuoli, port city for Naples]. There we found some brothers and were urged to stay with them for seven days. And thus we came to Rome. The brothers from there heard about us and came as far as the Forum of Appius and Three Taverns to meet us. On seeing them, Paul gave thanks to God and took courage. When he entered Rome, Paul was allowed to live by himself, with the soldier who was guarding him" (Acts 28:13b–16).

As we stand amidst the ruins of what might have been Three Taverns, take a moment to look around. Soak up the scenery. Look down the road to see if you can discern the image of ancient sojourners. Is it the slave of Atticus with news for Cicero? Is it a band of brothers coming to meet Paul? What news from Three Taverns will you write about?

Forum Appius
(Foro Appio)

It is supposed that the town of Forum Appius was founded in 312 BCE when the Appian Way was constructed. Eventually, this town marked the point at which travelers would move to a raft on the canal. Travelers could then sleep while the donkey pulled the raft down the canal. We are near the Pontine Marshes. Today, the town is also known as Borgo Faiti, on the Appian Way of course, near the modern town of Latina.

Horace (65–8 BCE), a writer of satire with friends in influential places, writes about a journey from Rome to Brundisium for the signing of a treaty (some scholars believe the meeting was that between Octavian and Antony in 38 BCE in Athens). In this descriptive account, called a "shaggy dog story" by one modern scholar,[23] the reader sees many various aspects of ancient Roman travel.

Here we end our journey, where Paul first met those from Rome (Acts 28:15) who would accompany him on his journey to the city where he would eventually die a martyr's death. In a sense, we've come full circle, starting at St. Peter's, the site of Peter's martyrdom and ending here where Paul first encountered those who might possibly have accompanied him to his death.

23. Gowers, "Horace, *Satires* 1.5," 66.

6

Synagogue and Environs

Synagogue

WHEN WE VISIT THE synagogue we are reminded of the deep roots of the Jewish community in Rome. Of course, it was most likely from this Jewish community that the first Christian community arose. It is unfortunate and deplorable then that in the heart of Christianity as it were such virulent anti-Semitism took root and grew. Only recently, after the Holocaust, has the Catholic Church officially condemned and removed traces of anti-Semitism from its liturgies and teaching.

At Vatican II, one of the last documents published, *Nostra Aetate* claimed,

> As the sacred synod searches into the mystery of the Church, it remembers the bond that spiritually ties the people of the New Covenant to Abraham's stock.
>
> Thus the Church of Christ acknowledges that, according to God's saving design, the beginnings of her faith and her election are found already among the Patriarchs, Moses and the prophets. She professes that all who believe in Christ-Abraham's sons according to faith-are included in the same Patriarch's call, and likewise that the salvation of the Church is mysteriously foreshadowed by the chosen people's exodus from the land of bondage. The Church, therefore, cannot forget that she received the revelation of the Old Testament through the people with whom God in His inexpressible mercy concluded the Ancient Covenant. Nor can she forget that she draws sustenance from the root of that well-cultivated olive tree onto which have been grafted the wild shoots, the

Gentiles. Indeed, the Church believes that by His cross Christ, Our Peace, reconciled Jews and Gentiles, making both one in Himself.

The Church keeps ever in mind the words of the Apostle about his kinsmen: "theirs is the sonship and the glory and the covenants and the law and the worship and the promises; theirs are the fathers and from them is the Christ according to the flesh" (Rom. 9:4–5), the Son of the Virgin Mary. She also recalls that the Apostles, the Church's main-stay and pillars, as well as most of the early disciples who proclaimed Christ's Gospel to the world, sprang from the Jewish people.

As Holy Scripture testifies, Jerusalem did not recognize the time of her visitation, nor did the Jews in large number, accept the Gospel; indeed not a few opposed its spreading. Nevertheless, God holds the Jews most dear for the sake of their Fathers; He does not repent of the gifts He makes or of the calls He issues-such is the witness of the Apostle. In company with the Prophets and the same Apostle, the Church awaits that day, known to God alone, on which all peoples will address the Lord in a single voice and "serve him shoulder to shoulder" (Soph. 3:9) [Zeph 3:9].

Since the spiritual patrimony common to Christians and Jews is thus so great, this sacred synod wants to foster and recommend that mutual understanding and respect which is the fruit, above all, of biblical and theological studies as well as of fraternal dialogues.

True, the Jewish authorities and those who followed their lead pressed for the death of Christ; still, what happened in His passion cannot be charged against all the Jews, without distinction, then alive, nor against the Jews of today. Although the Church is the new people of God, the Jews should not be presented as rejected or accursed by God, as if this followed from the Holy Scriptures. All should see to it, then, that in catechetical work or in the preaching of the word of God they do not teach anything that does not conform to the truth of the Gospel and the spirit of Christ.

Furthermore, in her rejection of every persecution against any man, the Church, mindful of the patrimony she shares with the Jews and moved not by political reasons but by the Gospel's spiritual love, decries hatred, persecutions, displays of anti-Semitism, directed against Jews at any time and by anyone.

Besides, as the Church has always held and holds now, Christ underwent His passion and death freely, because of the sins of men and out of infinite love, in order that all may reach salvation. It is, therefore, the burden of the Church's preaching to proclaim the cross of Christ as the sign of God's all-embracing love and as the fountain from which every grace flows.[1]

This statement was a tremendous move forward for a church that only years earlier, in the Good Friday liturgy, prayed for the "perfidious" Jews.

As Christians, it is important for us to recognize not only the Jewish roots of Christianity, but to face starkly the history of Christian persecution of Jews. We should not turn a blind eye to historical fact.

Briefly, the New Testament has many passages that can be understood in an anti-Jewish way, beginning with the earliest composition in the New Testament, Paul's First Letter to the Thessalonians:

> For you, brothers, have become imitators of the churches of God that are in Judea in Christ Jesus. For you suffer the same things from your compatriots as they did from the Jews, who killed both the Lord Jesus and the prophets and persecuted us; they do not please God, and are opposed to everyone, trying to prevent us from speaking to the Gentiles that they may be saved, thus constantly filling up the measure of their sins. But the wrath of God has finally begun to come upon them (1 Thess 2:14–16).

We wonder if Paul would have written these words in this occasional letter if he knew people all over the globe would be reading it two thousand years later. While he may have been aggravated at some of his fellow Jews who were hindering his work with the gospel, saying in a broad way that the Jews do not please God, that they are opposed to everyone, that they are filling up the measure of their sins so that the wrath of God is coming upon them, is harsh language indeed.

Besides this example from the New Testament (and there are others), the early Christian Fathers were often engaged in debate with Jews over the nature of Christ. Origen's *Against Celsus* and Justin Martyr's *Dialogue with Trypho* are only two such examples. Celsus was a historical figure who wrote an attack on Christianity from his own familiarity with Jewish thought; whereas Trypho was a Jewish character in a fictional dialogue with Justin. Unfortunately, some of the Christian Saints have also spouted forth vicious anti-Jewish remarks. For example, Saint Augustine says,

> But the Jews, who killed him [Jesus] and would not believe in him, because he must needs die and rise again, were ravaged still more

---

1. Nostra Aetate, 4. http://www.vatican.va/archive/hist_councils/ii_vatican_council/documents/vat-ii_decl_19651028_nostra-aetate_en.html

miserably by the Romans, and were utterly uprooted from their kingdom, where they had already been ruled by foreign-born rulers; and they were scattered throughout the lands,—for indeed there is no place where they are not found,—and so by means of their own Scriptures they bear witness on our behalf that we have not forged the prophecies about Christ. Very many of them, considering these prophecies both before his passion and still more after his resurrection, believed on him. Of them it was predicted: "Though the number of the sons of Israel be as the sand of the sea, the remnant shall be saved" [Isa 10:22; Rom 9:27]. But the rest were blinded; of them it was predicted: "Let their table be a trap in their presence and a retribution and a stumbling-block; let their eyes be darkened, that they may not see; and do thou bow down their backs always" [Ps 69:22; Rom 11:9–10]. Therefore, when they do not believe in our Scriptures, their own Scriptures, to which they are blind when they read, are fulfilled in them . . .

For a prophecy about this thing was given in advance, in the Psalms which they, too, read, where it is written: "My God, his mercy shall go before me; my God has shown me concerning my enemies, that you are not to slay them, lest they some day forget your law; scatter them by your might" [Ps 59:10–11]. So God has shown the church the grace of his mercy in the case of her enemies the Jews, since, as the Apostle says: "Their sin is the salvation of the Gentiles" [Rom 11:11]. For this reason he did not slay them (that is, he did not put an end to their being Jews, although they were conquered and oppressed by the Romans), lest through forgetting the law of God they should bear no effective witness on this point that we are concerned with. So it was not enough for him to say: "You are not to slay them, lest they some day forget your law," without also adding: "Scatter them." For if they dwelt with that testimony of their Scriptures in their own land only, and not everywhere, then the church, which is everywhere, could not have them at hand among all the Gentiles as witnesses to those prophecies that were given in advance concerning Christ.[2]

So, Augustine's contention is that by his time the Jews had been scattered upon the earth (i.e., the diaspora) and not utterly killed (genocide) because their presence throughout the world could keep and bear witness to the scriptures (Old Testament). That is, if the Jews had been killed so there was not one Jew left, Christians would not have an independent testimony to the prophecies in the scriptures. To many people today, this may

---

2. Augustine, *City of God*, 18.46.

sound like rather convoluted thinking and only a few short steps away from implicitly endorsing genocide.

One of Augustine's contemporaries, John Chrysostom (349–407), Archbishop of Constantinople has a series of eight homilies entitled, "Against the Jews." The name "Chrysostom" is Greek for "Golden-tongue." Chrysostom echoed Augustine in claiming that the Jews killed Jesus, though this Saint and Doctor of the church used his "golden tongue" to coin the term "Christ-killer" and apply it to Jews.[3] (Of course, only the Romans had the authority to put someone to death in Judea at the time Jesus was executed). The thinking of the church fathers, and perhaps the church in general, regarding the Jewish people is largely represented by Augustine and John Chrysostom. It is true that not each and every Christian would harbor such thoughts, but the leading Christian thinkers of the day did, and their ideas carried the day and carried influence a millennim later.

Christian attitudes towards Jews reached a critical point in the sixteenth century when Pope Paul IV (1476–1559) created the Jewish Ghetto in Rome with his Papal Bull, *Cum Nimis Absurdum* issued on July 14, 1555. The ghetto district was surrounded by walls with three gates, which were locked each night. Jewish men were required to wear yellow stars, and Jewish women, yellow handkerchiefs. A church at each gate proselytized to the Jews. In fact we can see one church, Santa Maria della Pietà near the Ponte Fabrizio. (In 2007 it experienced a facelift). If you can see the Hebrew and Latin script under the crucifix at the door you will notice that it is a quote from Isaiah 65:2–3a, which Paul cites in Romans 10:21. The Latin is reproduced here with an English translation:

> expandi manus meas tota die ad
>
> populum incredulum qui graditur
>
> in via non bona post cogitationes suas
>
> populus qui ad iracundiam provocat
>
> me ante faciem meam semper
>
> congregatio divina pietatis posuit
>
> I held out my hands all day long to
>
> an unbelieving people, who walk

---

3. E.g., John Chrysostom, "Against the Jews," Homily 6.2.10 in PG 48.905; 6.3.3 in PG 48.907.

in a way that is not good, following their own devices;

a people who are always provoking

me to my face.

The congregation for divine piety placed this here.

It is hard to believe the congregation for divine piety missed the blatant irony in setting up this inscription under the crucifix of a church stationed at the gate of the Jewish ghetto in Rome. The action seems anything but pious.

In many respects this anti-Semitism was unfortunately a feature of the Christianity of Paul IV's day. In other words, attitudes toward the Jews transcended reformation debates for Martin Luther (1483–1546) himself wrote, *On the Jews and their Lies.*

> What shall we Christians do with this rejected and condemned people, the Jews? Since they live among us, we dare not tolerate their conduct, now that we are aware of their lying and reviling and blaspheming. If we do, we become sharers in their lies, cursing and blasphemy. Thus we cannot extinguish the unquenchable fire of divine wrath, of which the prophets speak, nor can we convert the Jews. With prayer and the fear of God we must practice a sharp mercy to see whether we might save at least a few from the glowing flames. We dare not avenge ourselves. Vengeance a thousand times worse than we could wish them already has them by the throat. I shall give you my sincere advice:
>
> First to set fire to their synagogues or schools and to bury and cover with dirt whatever will not burn, so that no man will ever again see a stone or cinder of them. This is to be done in honor of our Lord and of Christendom, so that God might see that we are Christians, and do not condone or knowingly tolerate such public lying, cursing, and blaspheming of his Son and of his Christians. For whatever we tolerated in the past unknowingly—and I myself was unaware of it—will be pardoned by God. But if we, now that we are informed, were to protect and shield such a house for the Jews, existing right before our very nose, in which they lie about, blaspheme, curse, vilify, and defame Christ and us (as was heard above), it would be the same as if we were doing all this and even worse ourselves, as we very well know . . .
>
> Second, I advise that their houses also be razed and destroyed. For they pursue in them the same aims as in their synagogues. Instead they might be lodged under a roof or in a barn, like the gypsies. This will bring home to them that they are not masters in our country, as they boast, but that they are living in exile and in captivity, as they incessantly wail and lament about us before God.
>
> Third, I advise that all their prayer books and Talmudic writings, in which such idolatry, lies, cursing and blasphemy are taught, be taken from them.
>
> Fourth, I advise that their rabbis be forbidden to teach henceforth on pain of loss of life and limb. For they have justly forfeited the right to such an office by holding the poor Jews captive with the saying of Moses (Deuteronomy 17 [:10 ff.]) in which he commands them to obey their teachers on penalty of

death, although Moses clearly adds: "what they teach you in accord with the law of the Lord." Those villains ignore that. They wantonly employ the poor people's obedience contrary to the law of the Lord and infuse them with this poison, cursing, and blasphemy. In the same way the pope also held us captive with the declaration in Matthew 16 [:18], "You are Peter," etc, inducing us to believe all the lies and deceptions that issued from his devilish mind. He did not teach in accord with the word of God, and therefore he forfeited the right to teach.

Fifth, I advise that safe-conduct on the highways be abolished completely for the Jews. For they have no business in the countryside, since they are not lords, officials, tradesmen, or the like. Let them stay at home . . .

Sixth, I advise that usury be prohibited to them, and that all cash and treasure of silver and gold be taken from them and put aside for safekeeping. The reason for such a measure is that, as said above, they have no other means of earning a livelihood than usury, and by it they have stolen and robbed from us all they possess. Such money should now be used in no other way than the following: Whenever a Jew is sincerely converted, he should be handed one hundred, two hundred, or three hundred florins, as personal circumstances may suggest. With this he could set himself up in some occupation for the support of his poor wife and children, and the maintenance of the old or feeble. For such evil gains are cursed if they are not put to use with God's blessing in a good and worthy cause . . .

Seventh, I recommend putting a flail, an ax, a hoe, a spade, a distaff, or a spindle into the hands of young, strong Jews and Jewesses and letting them earn their bread in the sweat of their brow, as was imposed on the children of Adam (Gen 3 [:19]). For it is not fitting that they should let us accursed Goyim toil in the sweat of our faces while they, the holy people, idle away their time behind the stove, feasting and farting, and on top of all, boasting blasphemously of their lordship over the Christians by means of our sweat. No, one should toss out these lazy rogues by the seat of their pants. [4]

It was not until after the unification of Italy in the late nineteenth century, and particularly when Rome and the Papal States fell in 1870, with the forces of the Risorgimento and their belief in equality, that the Jewish ghetto was taken from papal authority, demolished, and became more

---

4. Luther, "On the Jews and Their Lies," 268–70, 272.

incorporated into the city with standard city blocks instead of walls. Jews of Rome were offered other, better real estate for their synagogue, but they chose instead to establish it here in the ghetto, on the site of the earlier synagogue. This "Synagogue of Emancipation" was completed in 1904, after only three years of work. From that point, Jews in Rome experienced some of the best conditions they had in centuries. But this was to be short-lived as the rise of Mussolini and the alliance with Hitler would prove, reaching a zenith in the deportation of Jews from Rome on October 18, 1943. At the time, Rome was under Nazi occupation. The commandant told the Jewish community that they would be safe if they turned over fifty kilograms of gold. Not only Jews but many in Rome contributed to that effort, which only delayed the inevitable. Over 2000 Jews were taken from Rome though it is said many more went into hiding throughout the city. Even so, of the 2000 nearly half were sent to Auschwitz. We are reminded that this "history" is fewer than one hundred years ago. It is no wonder that after World War II, and during Vatican II, the church took the necessary step of reexamining its relationship with the Jewish people.

In the wake of World War II, especially the holocaust, the Roman Catholic Church began a penetrating analysis of her own words and actions with respect to Jews. In the past fifty years, the church has written much (especially for students of scripture) including *The Jewish People and Their Sacred Scripture in the Christian Bible* (Pontifical Biblical Commission, 2002). But often actions speak louder than words, so it is significant that Pope John Paul II visited this very synagogue on April 13, 1986, becoming the first pope in history ever to set foot in a synagogue. His presentation delivered that day is entitled, The Roots of Anti-Judaism in the Christian Environment, and is available on the Vatican website.[5] It was at this visit that he referred to the Jewish people as our "elder brother" in faith. Since that time both Pope Benedict XVI and Pope Francis have also visited the synagogue in Rome.

We too will follow these recent popes into the Synagogue to explore the history of the Jewish people in Rome. We remember that Jesus was a Jew, his disciples and apostles were Jews, Peter and Paul were Jews, and that Jews are our elder brothers in faith. In some sense then, this visit to a twentieth-century synagogue is a visit to our deepest roots of faith.

---

5. http://www.vatican.va/jubilee_2000/magazine/documents/ju_mag_01111997_p-42x_en.html.

Saint Paul at the Regola
(San Paolo alla Regola)

Near the synagogue is a church which claims the legendary residence of Paul. Unfortunately it is rarely open so we are pressing our luck, or perhaps hoping against hope that we can make a visit. If it is closed, we can admire it from the outside. As it is not far from the synagogue, and holds a special place in the memory of the church; it is worth the short walk even if it is closed.

The church dates to the seventeenth century. Its name, regola, is a corruption of "renula" which itself is an abbreviated form of "arenula," meaning beach or sand. Arenula was the name of this district of ancient Rome, also known as the seventh (VII) district. The name is a reminder that in antiquity the banks of the Tiber stretched to this point.

Beyond the legend, there is eleventh-century evidence of this place being referred to as the Schola Pauli or San Paolo de Arenula with the church itself being called San Paolino. In the Middle Ages this area was known for commerce. The church was a center for the many guilds, which had altars dedicated to their profession in the church, including the tanners (e.g., Acts 18:3 mentions that Paul was a tentmaker, a profession closely associated with tanning).

The church eventually fell out of use until the renaissance. In the seventeenth century, it was given to the Third Regular Order of St. Francis of the Sicilian Nation. They set up the Collegium Siculum here, belonging to the Kingdom of the Two Sicilies. The Collegium grew to the point where the church needed to be rebuilt. It reopened in 1705 as a Greek cross designed church. The façade, which mentions the Third Order of St. Francis and the Collegium, was completed in 1721.

Thus, nothing more than legend associates this place with Paul. Acts of the Apostles concludes by telling us:

> When he entered Rome, Paul was allowed to live by himself, with the soldier who was guarding him. Three days later he called together the leaders of the Jews. When they had gathered he said to them, "My brothers, although I had done nothing against our people or our ancestral customs, I was handed over to the Romans as a prisoner from Jerusalem. After trying my case the Romans wanted to release me, because they found nothing against me deserving the death penalty. But when the Jews objected, I was obliged to appeal to Caesar, even though I had no accusation to make against

my own nation. This is the reason, then, I have requested to see you and to speak with you, for it is on account of the hope of Israel that I wear these chains."

They answered him, "We have received no letters from Judea about you, nor has any of the brothers arrived with a damaging report or rumor about you. But we should like to hear you present your views, for we know that this sect is denounced everywhere."

So they arranged a day with him and came to his lodgings in great numbers. From early morning until evening, he expounded his position to them, bearing witness to the kingdom of God and trying to convince them about Jesus from the law of Moses and the prophets. Some were convinced by what he had said, while others did not believe.

Without reaching any agreement among themselves they began to leave; then Paul made one final statement. "Well did the holy Spirit speak to your ancestors through the prophet Isaiah, saying: 'Go to this people and say: You shall indeed hear but not understand. You shall indeed look but never see. Gross is the heart of this people; they will not hear with their ears; they have closed their eyes, so they may not see with their eyes and hear with their ears and understand with their heart and be converted, and I heal them.' Let it be known to you that this salvation of God has been sent to the Gentiles; they will listen."

He remained for two full years in his lodgings. He received all who came to him, and with complete assurance and without hindrance he proclaimed the kingdom of God and taught about the Lord Jesus Christ (Acts 28:16–31).

At this stop one recalls the bravery, courage, fortitude, and determination of the early Christians, their relationship with Judaism, their belief in Jesus the Christ, and the ultimate sacrifice they made for that belief. What will be known of us in 2000 years' time? Will there be a day in the distant future when we too will be known as the early Christians, and a student will ask a professor, "was Vatican II before or after the Council of Chalcedon?" As we stand on the banks of the Tiber, linked to Paul, Peter, and the Jewish roots of the Church in Rome, after studying our faith and its history, processing through Roman streets led by the Vicar of Peter, what will be our story as we return to our homes across the ocean? How will we live our Christian faith in the midst of the world?

The Rome of Peter and Paul—Part II

Santa Maria in Via Lata

Like San Paolo in Regola, Santa Maria in Via Lata claims to be the place where Saint Paul lodged for two years, according to Acts 28:30–31. Another legend claims that the church was built over the house of the centurion who watched over Paul during his house arrest. And the church itself will report to modern visitors that it was the home of St. Luke, where Paul stayed for the two years he was in Rome. This last association seems to have been recognized by Pope Alexander VII in 1661. Excavations indicate that it was part of ancient storehouse facilities that were common in the area. Visitors can visit the crypt in late afternoons Tuesdays through Sundays.[6] The church itself is perhaps best known for the altar and alabaster columns built by Bernini.[7]

The Ancient Via Lata, literally "wide street" or "broad way" is today the Via del Corso. In antiquity, the Via Lata was a city street and became the Via Flaminia outside the city. The Via Flaminia ran straight, almost due North, crossing the Tiber by means of the Milvian bridge, and continuing North between the Tiber and the eastern hills, eventually reaching the Adriatic Sea. The Via Lata was marked by the Ara Pacis of Augustus, the Arch of Claudius, one of the arches of the Aqua Virgo aqueduct (remnants are still standing at No. 14 Via del Nazareno), and the Mausoleum of Augustus. Today, the transition between the Via del Corso and the Via Flaminia is the Piazza del Popolo.

---

6. For more current information, see http://www.cryptavialata.it/
7. Mason, *Companion Guide to Rome*, 85.

St. Peter in Montorio
(St. Pietro in Montorio)

The Tempietto by Bramante

San Pietro in Montorio[8] is a curious site in that it preserves a now little-known tradition that Peter was crucified here. The site itself was determined by the legend, which says that Peter was crucified *inter duas metas*,[9] "between two metae" (the obelisk markers that indicated the end of a circus race track). During the Renaissance, scholars interpreted the

---

8. As stated earlier, "Montorio" comes from the Classical Latin name for this hill: Mons Aureus (golden mountain).

9. For more on this see Part I of this book, the sections on the Acts of Peter and the *Acta Sanctorum*, and the piece about the Filarete Doors in the section on the Basilica of St. Peter.

two metae to be the Meta of Remus (now known as the Pyramide, or the tomb of Gaius Cestius)[10] and the Meta of Romulus (near the Vatican). The location of San Pietro in Montorio was the point between these two metae. Though the legend is in the much later *Acta Sanctorum*, we know from looking at the Filarete Doors on St. Peter's Basilica, that the legend was prevalent then (fourteenth century). Moreover, Biondo mentions the legend too, though he dismisses the idea that Peter was crucified on the Janiculum (Mons Aureus).[11]

The medieval church was rebuilt in the late fifteenth century by Ferdinand and Isabella of Spain.[12] The surrounding area and the church itself saw fierce fighting in 1849, during the Risorgimento, as Garibaldi made his defense of the Roman Republic on this hill against the French troops commanded by Nicolas Oudinot. Restoration work on the apse and campanile was done in 1851.

Interesting artwork in the church includes "The conversion of Saint Paul" by Vasari in the semicircular chapel on the right transept. Vasari includes himself in the painting; look for the figure in black on the left. The church also has a copy of Reni's "Crucifixion of St. Peter" in the central apse. The painting takes the place of Raphael's transfiguration, which hung here from 1523 to 1809, when Napoleon took it as booty. It and the Reni original are now in the Vatican Museum.[13]

From the church, one can exit into the cloister, where Bramante built his masterpiece, the Tempietto (1502–7). Bernini added the staircase later. The Tempietto is a perfection of harmony and balance with its sixteen columns, dome, and circular structure. The crypt of the Tempietto commemorates the supposed precise location of Peter's martyrdom.

---

10. See footnote 42 on page 24.

11. Huskinson, "The Crucifixion of St. Peter," 135–61. Cf. Huskinson, Review of *Est et alia pyramis*, 618–21.

12. Technically, Ferdinand was King of Aragon and Isabella was Queen of Castile.

13. This section on San Pietro in Montorio is based on the information found in Masson, *The Companion Guide to Rome*, 529–32 and Macadam and Barber, *Rome*, 402–5.

Appendices

Churches

Four Basilicas

    St. Peter

    Saint John Lateran

    Saint Mary Major

    Saint Paul Outside the Walls

Seven Pilgirim Churches

    Four Basilicas (above)

    Saint Laurence Outside the Walls

    Santa Croce in Gerusalemme

    Saint Sebastian Outside the Walls (Pope John Paul II replaced Saint Sebastian with the Shrine of Our Lady of Divine Love in the year of the Great Jubilee, 2000.)

APPENDICES

Hills of Rome

Seven Hills of Rome
- Aventine Hill
- Caelian Hill
- Capitoline Hill
- Esquiline Hill
- Palatine Hill
- Quirinal Hill
- Viminal Hill

Other Hills of Rome
- Cispian Hill
- Janiculum Hill
- Mario Hill
- Oppian Hill
- Pincian Hill
- Testaccian Hill
- Vatican Hill
- Velian Hill

APPENDICES

The Station Churches

	Ash Wednesday	Santa Sabina
	Thursday	San Giorgio al Velabro
	Friday	Santi Giovanni e Paolo
	Saturday	Sant' Agostino
Week I	Sunday	San Giovanni in Laterano
	Monday	San Pietro in Vincoli
	Tuesday	Sant' Anastasia
	Wednesday	Santa Maria Maggiore
	Thursday	San Lorenzo in Panisperna
	Friday	Santi XII Apostoli
	Saturday	San Pietro in Vaticano
Week II	Sunday	Santa Maria in Domnica
	Monday	San Clemente
	Tuesday	Santa Balbina
	Wednesday	Santa Cecilia in Trastevere
	Thursday	Santa Maria in Trastevere
	Friday	San Vitale
	Saturday	Santi Marcellino e Pietro
Week III	Sunday	San Lorenzo fuori le mura
	Monday	San Marco
	Tuesday	Santa Pudenziana
	Wednesday	San Sisto
	Thursday	Santi Cosma e Damiano
	Friday	San Lorenzo in Lucina
	Saturday	Santa Susanna

Week IV	Sunday	Santa Croce in Gerusalemme
	Monday	Santi Quattro Coronati
	Tuesday	San Lorenzo in Damaso
	Wednesday	San Paolo fuori le mura
	Thursday	San Martino ai Monti
	Friday	Sant' Eusebio
	Saturday	San Nicola in Carcere
Week V	Sunday	San Pietro in Vaticano
	Monday	San Crisogono
	Tuesday	Santa Maria in Via Lata
	Wednesday	San Marcello
	Thursday	Sant' Apollinare
	Friday	Santo Stefano Rotonda
	Saturday	San Giovanni a Porta Latina
Holy Week	Palm Sunday	San Giovanni in Laterano
	Monday	Santa Prassede
	Tuesday	Santa Prisca
	Wednesday	Santa Maria Maggiore

APPENDICES

Important Sacks/Sieges/Occupations of Rome

390 BCE The Gauls

410 CE Rome sacked by Visigoths, King Alaric

455 CE Rome sacked by vandals

546 CE Ostrogoths

593 CE Besieged by the Lombards

846 CE Saracens looted St. Peter's Basilica and desecrated the site of Peter's tomb.

1084 CE Normans sack Rome (Robert Guiscard)

1527 CE Troops of Charles V (Holy Roman Emperor)

1797 CE Napoleon

1943 CE Nazis

APPENDICES

Roman Emperors

(from Augustus to Constantine, and with Theodosius and his son; regnal years)

Augustus	27 BCE–14 CE
Tiberius	14–37 CE
Caligula	37–41
Claudius	41–54
Nero	54–68
Galba	68–69
Otho	69
Vitellius	69
Vespasian	69–79
Titus	79–81
Domitian	81–96
Nerva	96–98
Trajan	98–117
Hadrian	117–38
Antoninus Pius	138–61
Marcus Aurelius	161–80
Commodus	180–92
Pertinax	193
Didus Iulianus	193
Septimius Severus	193–211
Caracalla	211–17
Opellius Macrinus	217–18
Elagabalus	218–22
Severus Alexander	222–35
Maximius	235–38
Gordian III	238–44
Philip	244–49

APPENDICES

Decius	249–51
Trebonius	251–53
Valerianus	253–60
Gallenius	253–68
Claudius Gothicus	268–70
Aurelian	270–75
Tacitus	275–76
Probus	276–82
Carus	282–83
Diocletian	284–305
Maximian	286–305
Constantius	292–302
Galerius	293–311
Licinius	311–23
Constantine	306–37

Theodosius (the Great)	379–95
Theodosius II (Eastern Emperor)	408–50

APPENDICES

Popes

(Only those mentioned in the book; dates are the Vatican's official list)

St. Peter	42–67
St. Linus	67–76
St. Clement I	88–97
St. Soter	166–75
St. Zephyrinus	199–217
St. Callistus	217–22
Liberius	352–66
St. Damasus	366–84
St. Gregory I (The Great)	590–604
St. Leo III	795–816
St. Paschal I	817–24
Innocent IV	1243–54
Boniface VIII	1295–1303
Eugenius IV	1431–47
Nicholas V	1447–55
Julius II	1503–13
Leo X	1513–21
Paul IV	1555–59
Clement VIII	1592–1605
Paul V	1605–21
Urban VIII	1623–44
Alexander VII	1655–69
Pius VII	1800–23
Pius IX	1846–78
Leo XIII	1878–1903
St. John Paul II	1978–2005
Benedict XVI	2005–13
Francis	2013–present

APPENDICES

The Passion of the Saints Processus and Martinianus, Martyrs.[1]

PASSIO SANCTORVM PROCESSI ET MARTINIANI MATYRVM

Tempore quo Symon magus crepuit: et impiissimus Nero tradidit beatissimos apostolos Christi Petrum et Paulum Paulino uiro benigno. Magister potestatis Paulinus mancipauit beatissimos apostolos in custodia Mamertini: ueniebantque ad eos multi e christianis infirmi: et a suis curabantur infirmitatibus: atque alii a daemonibus 10 liberabantur per orationes apostolorum. Erant autem custodientes eosdem beatissimos apostolos multi milites: inter quos duo magistri principes fuere Processus et Martinianus Hi cum uiderent mirabilia: quae faciebat per beatissimos apostolos suos dominus Iesus Christus: mirari coeperunt dicentes: Viri uenerabiles nostis: quia hic imperator Nero iam in obluuione processit a persona uestra ecce enim 15 nouem menses sunt quod in custodia estis. Rogamus itaque uos: ut ambuletis: quo uolueritis in huius nomine: in cuius uos cognouimus facere uirtutes magnas baptizate nos. Tunc dixerunt eis beatissimi apostoli Petrus et Paulus: Vos credite et omni eorde et mente uestra in nomine trinitatis: et uos ipsi potestis facere: quae nos facere cognouistis. Hoc audientes omnes qui in custodia erant: clamauerunt unanimiter 20 dicentes: donate nobis aquam: quia siti periclitamur. Eadem autem hora beatissimus Petrus in ipsa custodia Mamertini dum esset: dixit ad omnes. Credite in deum patrem omnipotentem et in Iesum Christum filium eius dominum unigenitum et in spiritum sanctum: et omnia ministrabuntur uobis. Eadem autem hora miserunt se omnes ad pedes apostolorum rogantes: ut baptismum ab eis accipiant. 25 At uero beatissimi apostoli orauerunt in eadem custodia: Cunque orrasent: illico beatus Petrus apostolus facto signo Crucis iu monte Tarpeio in custodia Mamertini eadem hora emanauerunt aquae de monte. Tune baptizati sunt beatus processus et Martinianus magistriani principes a beato Petro apostolo. Hoc dum uidissent cuncti: qui in custodia erant: Prostrauerunt se ad pedes beati Petri apostoli: || et baptizati 30 sunt promiscui sexus et aetatis numero quinquagintaseptem. Tunc obtulit pro eis sacrificium laudis: et participati sunt omnes corpore et sanguine domini nostri Iesu Christi. Uidentes autem beati Processus et Martinianus magistri dixerunt ad sanctos apostolos Christi Petrum et Paulum: Pergite quo desyderatis:

---

1. Mombrizio, *Sanctuarium seu Vitae Sanctorum*, 2:403–4.

APPENDICES

quia oblitus Nero desperauit de uobis. Exeuntes uero de custodia sancti apostoli Petrus et Paulus uenerunt 35 per uiam: quae Appia nuncupatur: et coeperunt peruenire usque ad portam Appiam. Tunc beatissimus Petus dum tibiam demolitam haberet de compede ferri cedite ei fasciola ante septem solium in uia noua. Eodem autem tempore ueniens iuxta portam Appiam uidit dominum Iesum: quem cognoscens dixit ei Petrus: domine quo pergis? Et dominus inquit: Romam redeo iterum crucifigi tu autem redi Romam. Et rediit 40 Petrus Romam: Cunque rediret mane: ecce magistriani tenuerunt eum. Eodem uero tempore nunciatum est Paulino uiro clarissimo magistro officii: eo quod Processus et Martinianus magistriani christiani effecti fuerant, misit milites et tenuit eos:et iussit in custodiam recludi. Alia autem die praecepit eos sibi praesentari. Qui cum adducti fuissent: dixit eis Paulinus: Sic stulti facti estis ut deserentes deos et deas: quas 45 inuictissimi principes Colunt: et antiquitas nostra adorat: sequi uelitis uana et mendacia? Respondit Martnianus clara uoce et dixit: Nos modo coepimus habere sacramenta militiae caelestic. Paulinus dixit: deponite iam amentiam cordis uestri: Et adorante deos inmortales: quos a cunabulis uestris uenerati estis. Beati martyres Processus et Martinianus respondentes: una uoce dixeront: Nos christiani facti 50 sumus. Dixit autem ad eos Paulinus: Audite me commilitones mei: et facite quae dico: et estote amici mei: fruiminique militia uestra: et estote clari principum: et sacrificate diis omnipotentibus: et uiuite: respondentes ambo simul tanquam ex uno [page 404] ore dixerunt ei: Sufficit nos declarare tibi: quia christiani ueraces sumus et serui dei et domini nostri Iesu Christi: quem beatissimi apostolic eius Petrus Cum Paulo praedicauerunt. Paulinus | igitur dixit: Iam dixi uobis. Et audistis et nunc iterum dicouobis: Audite consilium meum: et uiuite. Illi autem tacuerunt. Iterum autem atque 5 iterum interrogauit eos Paulinis: Et iussit ut cum lapidibus tunc ora eorum contunderentur: Cumque diu caederentur: Cumque diu caederantur: Clamabant ambo partier dicentes: Gloria in excelsis deo: et in terra pax hominibus bone uoluntatis. Paulinus uero dixit militibus suis: Proferte modo tripoda: et thurificent maiestatibus. Beati igitur martyres Processus et Martinianus hoc audientes dixerunt: Nosmetipsos semel obtulimus deo omnipotenti. 10 Et allata tripoda dixit eis: facite quae dico: Et detulerunt Iouem aureum. Hoc autem cum uiderent: risum facientes: expuerunt in Iouem et tripodam coram Paulino magistro officii. Iterum autem idem Paulinus praecepit eos in equuleo suspendi: et attrahi neruis et caedi fustibus. Illi autem uultu alacri gaudentes dicebant: Gratias tibi agimus domine Iesu Christe. Paulinus nimio furore accensus iussit 15 ut flamas ponerent circa latera eorum. Illi autem uociferabant benedictum nomen domini nostri Iesu Christi: quem beatissimi apostoli eius Petrus et Paulus praedicauerunt. Erat autem ibi quaedam matrona nobilissima foemina nomine Lucina: quae ante illos stabat et eos confortabat: dicebatque eis: Milites Christi nolite metuere poenas:quae ad tempus sunt. Paulinus ad eos dixit: Quae est ista amentia uestra? Illi autem 20 corroborati deridebant tormenta. iussit itaque militibus: ut scorpionibus eos appensos in equuleo castigarent sub uoce praeconia dicentes: praecepta principum contemnere nolite. Eadem autem hora Paulinis magister officii amisit oculum sinistrum ex quo poenitentia ductus prae timore et dolore. Coepit clamare: oh carmina artis magicae praecepit que eos deponi de equuleo: et diu maceratos retrudi in custodia Mamertini 25 Matrona autem uenerahlis Luciana incessanter ministrabat sanctis martyribus in custodia: post triduum autem Paulinis subito a daemonio arreptus expirauit. Tunc filius eius Pampinius coepit clamare ad palatium pergens: moderators et gubernatores reipublicae uestra subuenite: ut extinguantur magicae artis induti: Haec audiens Praefectus Urbis Caesarius intimauit Neroni augusto tem || gestam. Nero autem 30 imperator praecepit dicens. Non tardentur: sed celerius extinguantur. Pompinius uero magistri officci filius coepit fortiter urgere praefectum Urbis Caesarium: Quare ille lata sententia: iussuit eos eiici de custodia: et duci foras muros urbis Romae: in uiam: quae Aurelia nuncupatur: et ibi capite gladio sunt amputati. Beatissima autem Lucina cum hoc uideret: sequebatur eos cum familia sua: usque dum peruenirent iuxta 35 formam aquaeductus: ubi etiam decolati sunt: et corpora eorum relicta sunt truncata a canibus deuoranda sanctissima uero foemina lucina collegit corpora eorum: et condiuit cum aromatibus pretiosis: sepeliutque in praedio suo in harenario iuxta locum: ubi decolati sunt sub die sexto nonas iulias uia Aurelia : ubi praestantur beneficia eorum usque in diem hunc: Regnante domino nostro Iesu Christo: qui 40 uiuit et regnat deus in unitate spiritussancti per omnia saecula saeculorum. Amen.

At the time when Simon Magus raised a ruckus, and the most impious Nero handed over the most blessed apostles of Christ, Peter and Paul, to Paulinus, a kind man, the commander Paulinus transferred the most blessed apostles to the Mamertine prison. And many sick from the Christians were coming to them and they were cured of their infirmities, and others were freed from evil spirits through the prayers of the apostles.

However, many soldiers were guarding the same most blessed apostles, among whom were two guards, Processus and Martinianus. When they saw the wonders which the Lord Jesus Christ was doing through his most blessed apostles they began to marvel saying, "Venerable men you know that the Emperor Nero has by now forgotten about you. Truly, it is the ninth month that you have been in prison. So we ask you to baptize us, and you may walk where you wish in this name in which we know you have done great works." Then the most blessed apostles Peter and Paul said to them, "If you will believe with your whole heart and your mind in the name of the Trinity, then you yourselves will be able to do what you know we do." When all those who were in the prison heard this they cried out unanimously saying, "Give us this water for we are dying of thirst."

At that same hour the most blessed Peter, while he was in the Mamertine prison, said to all, "Believe in God the Father almighty and in Jesus Christ his only son, the Lord, and in the Holy Spirit, and all will be done for you." At the same hour they all placed themselves at the feet of the apostles asking to receive baptism from them (26). And indeed, the most blessed apostles prayed in that very prison. And when they were praying, in that place the blessed apostle Peter made the sign of the cross on the Tarpeian hill in the Mamertine prison, at that very time waters flowed from the hill. Then the blessed Processus and Martinianus, the chief guards, were baptized by the blessed apostle Peter.

When all who were in the prison saw this, they prostrated themselves at the feet of the blessed Apostle Peter. They were baptized, a mix of gender and age, to the number of fifty-seven. Then they offered for them the sacrifice of praise. And they all participated in the body and blood of our Lord Jesus Christ (33). So, seeing this, the blessed teachers Processus and Martinianus said to the holy apostles Peter and Paul, "Go wherever you desire. Because forgetful Nero has given up on you." So leaving the prison, the holy apostles Peter and Paul went out along the way known as Appia. And they came to the Appian gate. Then the most blessed Peter, while he had a severely injured leg from the iron shackles, removed the bandage before the seven stone coffins on the Via Nova.

At that very time, coming next to the Appian gate he saw the Lord Jesus, whom Peter recognized and said to him, "Lord, where are you going?" (*domine, quo pergis?*) (39). And the Lord answered, "I am going back to Rome to be crucified again. However, you go back to Rome." And Peter went back to Rome. And when he had gone back in the morning, behold the soldiers took hold of him.

Indeed, at that very time it was announced to most noble Paulinus, drill-instructor, that Processus and Martinianus, once instructed, had been made Christians. He sent soldiers and apprehended them. And he ordered them to be thrown into prison. However on another day he ordered them to present themselves [for trial]. And when they appeared before him Paulinus said to them, "Have you become so stupid that you fail to recognize the gods and goddesses which the invincible emperors worship, and our ancestors adored, and that you follow lies and vanity? (47). Martinianus responded with a clear voice and said, "We have recently begun to take our oath of allegiance to the army of heaven." Paulinus said, "Now put aside the madness of your heart, and worship the immortal gods whom you have venerated from your infancy."

The blessed martyrs Processus and Martinianus responding said with one voice, "We have been made Christians." However, Paulinus said to them, "Hear me my fellow soldiers and do what I say and be my friends and enjoy your service, and be noble leaders! (53). And sacrifice to the omnipotent gods and live." Both responding at the same time with one mouth said to him, "It is enough for us to say to you: we are true Christians and servants of our God and Lord Jesus Christ, whom his most blessed apostles Peter with Paul preached."

Paulinus therefore said, "So I have already spoken to you and you have listened. And now I say to you again, "Hear my advice and live." They however were silent. So again and again Paulinus interrogated them, and he ordered that their mouths be pounded with stones. While they were being severely beaten they both cried out alike saying, "Glory to God in the highest and on earth peace to those of goodwill."

Paulinus said to his soldiers, "Bring forth the tripod and they will burn incense to the majesties." The blessed martyrs Processus and Martinianus hearing this said, "We have offered our very selves once-for-all to almighty God." When the tripod was delivered he said to them, "Do what I say" (10). And they brought the golden (statue of) Jupiter. When they saw it they began to mock it. They spit on the Jupiter and the tripod in the presence of Paulinus, the drill-instructor.

So Paulinus again ordered them to be hung on the rack, their joints stretched and beaten with sticks. They however looked happy and rejoicing said, "We give thanks to you Lord Jesus Christ." Paulinus, now that his anger was exceedingly kindled, order that fire be applied to their sides. However they cried out, "Blessed be the name of the Lord, Jesus Christ, whom his most blessed apostles Peter and Paul preached."

Now, there was a most noble lady by the name of Lucina who stood before them and comforted them. She said to them, "Soldiers of Christ do not be afraid of the punishment that is but for a time." Paulinus said to them, "What is this insanity of yours?" Thus strengthened they laughed at the torments. So he gave orders to the soldiers that they be chastised with scorpions, suspending them on the rack, and with a loud voice saying, "Do not despise the commands of the leaders."

At that very hour, Paulinus, drill-instructor, lost his left eye; because of this punishment led by fear and pain, he began to shout, "Oh the spells of the magic art!" And he charged them to be placed on the rack. And he charged that after they were tortured at length, they be returned to the Mamertine prison. However the venerable matron Lucina was unceasingly ministering to the holy martyrs in prison. After three days Paulinus, seized by a demon, suddenly died.

Then his son Pompinius, going to the palace, began to shout, "Officers and governors of your republic, help! Let these dealers of the magic art be eradicated!" Hearing this, Caesarius, prefect of the city, reported the matter to Nero Augustus in short order. The emperor Nero ordered saying, "Do not delay! But eradicate them quickly!"

In response, Pompinius, the son of the drill-instructor began to strongly urge Caesarius, the prefect of the city. Therefore, that one passed sentence [upon them]. He ordered them to be brought out from the prison and to be led outside the walls of the city of Rome on the road that is called Aurelia. And there they were decapitated with a sword. When the most blessed Lucina saw this she followed them with her family until they arrived at the form of the aqueduct where they were beheaded and the trunks of their bodies were left, to be devoured by dogs. The most holy woman Lucina gathered their bodies and preserved them with valuable spices. And she buried [them] on her estate in a sandpit next to the place where they were beheaded on the sixth of the Nones of July on the Aurelian Way, where their favors are bestowed to this day, while our lord Jesus Christ reigns, who lives and reigns, God, in the unity of the Holy Spirit for all ages of ages.

APPENDICES

Abbreviations on Inscriptions in Rome[2]
(Rev. Patrick J. Madden, PhD)
Latin, unless marked as Italian (It.) or Greek (Gk.)

Sometimes abbreviations have a period after them;
sometimes they have a line above them.

A.	Ab	from, by (agent)
A.	Anno	In the year
A.D.	Anno Domini	In the year of (our) Lord
AN.	Anno	in the year
A.U.C	Ab Urbe Condita	from the foundation of the city (753 BCE)
ANN.	Anno	In the year
BASIL.	Basilicae	Of (this) basilica
C.	Condita	founded
C.	Gaius, Gaia	Roman names
C.	Censor	Censor (Roman official)
C.	Consul	Consul (high Roman official)
CAES.	Caesari	[dedicated] to Caesar
Car.	Cardinalis	Cardinal
Card.	Cardinalis	Cardinal
Cos	Cocceius	a Roman name
D.	Deo	to God
D.	Domini	of (our) Lord
D.M.	Dis Manibus	[dedicated/sacred] to the departed spirit(s)[3]
D.M.S.	Dis Manibus Sacrum	Sacred to the departed spirits

2. Abbreviates have been checked with a dictionary. All meanings for the abbreviation are given, not just the meaning in the inscription which prompted the "look-up."

3. *Manēs* has no singular, so it can be rendered "spirit," or "spirits" if there is more than one person in the tomb. This would be a pagan inscription, not a Christian one.

APPENDICES

D.O.M.	Dis Optimis Maximis	to the gods, the greatest, the best (pagan)
D.O.M.	Deo Optimo Maximo	to God, the best, the greatest (Christian)
IHS	Iesus (Gk.)	Jesus
F.	Felici	[dedicated] to Felix (= the fortunate one) (on the Arch of Constantine)
F.	Filio	[dedicated] to the son (on the Arch of Titus)
FL	Flaviano	[dedicated] to Flavius
H.M.H.N.S.	Hoc monumentum heredem non sequetur	This monument (tomb) will not belong to [my] heir.
I.N.R.I	Iesus Nazarenus Rex Iudaeorum	Jesus of Nazareth, King of the Jews
IMP	Imperatori	[dedicated] to the Emperor
IMP · CAES ·	Imperatori Caesari	[dedicated] to the Emperor Caesar
IMP · CAES · FL	Imperatorio Caesari Flavio	[dedicated] to the Emperor Flavius Caesar
IS.	Iesus	Jesus
IOHS	Iohannes	John
L.	Lucius	a Roman name
L.	libens	freely
L.	locus	place
L.	libertus	a freedman
M.	Marcus	Mark, a Roman name
M.	magister	master, teacher
M.	monumentum	monument
M.	municipium	township
MART.	Martyri	to the martyr
NRI	Nostri	Of Our

APPENDICES

P.	Pontifiex	Pontiff (= bridge-builder)
P.	Publius	a Roman name
P.	parte	in part, partially
P.	pater	father
P.	pedes	feet
P.	pio	[dedicated] to the "pious" = loyal, not holy
P.	pondo	in weight, with a weight of
P.	populus	people
P.	posuerunt	they placed
P.	publicus	public
P.C.	patres conscripti	"conscript fathers" = senators
P.C.	patronus civitatis / coloniae	patron of the city/colony
P.C.	ponendum curavit	he took care of the placement
P.C.	potestate censoria	with the power of the Censor
P.M.	Pontifiex Maximus	Supreme Pontiff (chief bridge builder)
P.M.	patronus minicipii	patron of the township
P.M.	posuit merito	He worthily placed
P.P.	pater patriae	father of the country/fatherland
P.P.	primus pilus	"first spear," = chief centurion
P.R.	Populus Romanus	The Roman People
P.S.	Pecunia Sua	His own money
Pont.	Pontifex	Pontiff, bridge-builder
Pont. Max	Pontifiex Maximus	Supreme Pontiff
Pontus.	Pontificatus	Pontificate
Pont. Nri.	Pontificatus Nostri	Of our Pontificate
PPHA	Propheta	Prophet
Pres.	Presbyterus	Presbyter
PSO	Praesto	I (this monument) present
Q.	Quintus	a Roman name
Q.	quaestor	a Roman official
Q.	Que	and (at the end of a word)
Q.V.A.	qui vixit annos ____	who lived ____ years

APPENDICES

R.	Romanus, a, um	Roman
S.	Sanctus, a, um,	Saint, Holy Man
S.	Senatus	Senate
S.	Sextus	
S.	suffectus	suffect (= holding office at the same time)
S.C.	suffecti consuli	suffect consuls
S.P.Q.R.	Senatus Populus Que Romanus	The Senate and the Roman People
S.R.E	Sanctae Romanae Ecclesiae	of the Holy Roman Church
S.R.E. Card	S.R.E. Cardinalis	Cardinal of the Holy Roman Church
S.R.E. Pres	S.R.E. Presbyterus	Presbyter of the Holy Roman Church
SSMA	Sanctissima (It.)	Most Holy (same as Latin)
Sta.	Sancta, Santa (It.)	Saint, Holy Woman
S.T.T.L.	Sit Terra Tibi Levis	May the earth rest lightly upon you.
T.	Titus	a Roman name
T. F.	Testamenti Formula	Formulation of a Testament / Will
T.F.C.	Titulum Faciendum Curavit	He took care of making the title (sign)
Ti	Tiberius	a Roman name
TI.	Titulus	Title (official assignment, appointment)
TI. BASIL.	Titulus huius basilicae	Title of this Basilica
T.P.	Tribunica potestatis	The authority of the tribune
TR	Tribunus	Tribune (Roman official)
U.	Urbe	city
XS HS	Christus Iesus (Gk.)	Christ Jesus

APPENDICES

Omissions

| [] | fecerunt | made |
| [] | posuerunt | placed, erected, set up |

Because they can be so easily supplied, words like *fēcērunt* and *posuērunt* are frequently omitted, as in the inscription

> Dis Manibus Gaji Plinii Valeriani medici, qui vixit annis viginti duobus (XXII), mensibus sex, diebus quinque, parentes [fecerunt / posuerunt].

> To the departed spirit of Gaius Plinius Valerianus, a physician, who lived 22 years, 6 months, 15 days, [his] parents [have erected this monument.][4]

Roman Numerals

I	1
V	5
X	10
L	50
C	100
D	500
M	1000

Rules for reading Roman Numerals

When an equal or a lesser number is to the right, it is added to the number on its left

$$II = 1 + 1 = 2$$
$$VI = 5 + 1 = 6$$
$$VII = 5 + 1 + 1 = 7$$
$$LXI = 50 + 10 + 1 = 61$$
$$MM = 1000 + 1000 = 2000$$

---

4. Sweet, *Lectiones Secundae*, 6–7. English translation is Madden's.

APPENDICES

When a lesser number is to the left, it is subtracted from the greater number on its right
$$IV = 5 - 1 = 4$$

If the last number in the series is the smallest, there is "no problem."

If the second-to-last number in a series is smaller than the last one, calculate these two together before adding to the rest.

$$XXIV = 10 + 10 + (5 - 1) = 24$$

MDCCCCLXXXXIX (from the inscription at St. Pietro in Montorio)

$$M + D + C + C + C + C + L + X + X + X + X + (X - I)$$

1000 + 500 + 100 +100 +100 + 100 + 50 + 10 + 10 +10 +10 + (10 − 1) = 1999

APPENDICES

Glossary of Terms

Apse	semicircular recess covered by a hemispherical vault.
Atrium	large open space within a building.
Baldachin	a ceremonial canopy over an altar.
Basilica	Roman public building. Meaning later came to be associated with a church.
Campus Martius	Field of Mars, an ancient flood plain for the Tiber, used often for military exercises in the Republican period. In the Imperial age it was a place for theaters, naumachiae, and other public uses. Today the Pantheon, Piazza Navona, and Pantheon mark the site of the ancient Campus Martius.
Carrara (marble)	city/environs in Tuscany known since antiquity for its high quality white marble quarried there. The modern city of Carrara was founded by the Ancient Romans as a village for the quarry workers.
Catacomb	Underground caves, passages for human burial, often with niches for the corpses.
Colonnade	Sequence of columns sometimes in pairs or sets of pairs, often joined by a horizontal feature, which is called an entablature.
Confessio	Niche for relics often found near the altar.
Consul	Title of the two chief magistrates of Rome, who served by election annually. The highest office of the state in the Republican era. Still functioned in the age of the empire, though subject to the emperor, who often served as consul. When a consul died in office a suffect (substitute) consul was named to take his place.
Entablature	The horizontal feature which joins a colonnade/columns and the pediment. The entablature is made up of the architrave (bottom), the frieze (middle), and the cornice (top).

APPENDICES

Façade — Ornamental front part of a church that often was not part of the original church itself.

Fresco — Style of art where the artist paints on wet plaster.

Frieze — A horizontal band of decoration on the entablature.

Mithraeum — Space dedicated to the worship of Mithras.

Mithras (or Mithra) — Persian god.

Mosaic — Style of art wherein the artist assembles small shards of stone, glass, or tile, set in grout.

Narthex — Part of a church that forms the entrance, or foyer.

Naumachia — The name for a mock sea battle, or the place where mock sea battles were staged. Plural is naumachiae.

Nave — The long aisle of a church leading from narthex to altar. The word is from the Latin term for "ship."

Nimbus — Disc or halo around the head of one depicted in artwork. A square or rectangular nimbus indicated that the person depicted was still alive at the time, whereas a round nimbus indicated the person was deceased.

Pallium — Religious garment given to a metropolitan archbishop at the Feast of Peter and Paul, June 29.

Pentelic (marble) — Penteli is mountain near Athens used a source of marble in antiquity, and even today. Pentelic marble is known for its purity.

Porphyry — Igneous rock with large grain crystals such as quartz. Porphyry is Greek for "purple." Porphyry was the hardest, most durable rock known in antiquity and was therefore used for many monuments.

Quadriga — Four-horse chariot often in bronze/marble atop arches or other monuments.

Sibyl — Ancient prophetess thought to deliver oracles.

APPENDICES

Transept   The part of a church that forms an aisle perpendicular to the nave.

Tufa   Soft, yet strong volcanic stone found throughout central Italy.

Glossary of Persons (Names)
In alphabetical order

Agrippina (the elder)   (14 BCE–33 CE) Granddaughter of Augustus, husband of Germanicus, and mother of Caligula. Namesake of the gardens in Ager Vaticana.

Agrippina (the younger)   (15–59 CE) great granddaughter of Augustus, sister of Caligula, niece and fourth wife of Claudius, and mother of the Emperor Nero.

Augustus (Caesar)   See "Octavian."

Barberini   A noble Florentine family that rose to prominence in Rome in the seventeenth century, culminating in the election of Pope Urban VIII (Cardinal Maffeo Barberini). Urban VIII hired Bernini for a number of projects in and around St. Peter's as well as for his family.

Bernini, Gian Lorenzo   (1598–1680) sculptor and architect who founded the Baroque style. Principal architect of St. Peter's for more than half his life. His works in Rome include the piazza at St. Peter's with its colonnade, the baldachin, chair of St. Peter, the Blessed Sacrament chapel, and more at St. Peter's. Some of his sculptures include, David, Ecstasy of St. Theresa, Apollo and Daphne, and the Rape of Proserpina. His works adorn the Eternal City and are too numerous to mention here.

APPENDICES

Borghese (Burghese)	A noble Sienese family that rose to prominence in Rome in the sixteenth and seventeenth centuries, highlighted by the election of Pope Paul V (Cardinal Camillo Borghese). The family continued to play a role on the international stage (to this day) and is perhaps best known in Rome for the Borghese gardens.
Bramante, Donato	(1444–1514) architect who was responsible for the Tempietto (St. Pietro in Montorio), which earned him the commission to "renovate" the Basilica of St. Peter's. Bramante lived long enough to see only the demolition, earning the nickname, "Bramante ruinante," (Bramante the destroyer).
Cambio, Arnolfo di	(ca. 1245–1310) architect and sculptor known for designing many works in Rome including the ciborium over the high altar at St. John Lateran, the bronze St. Peter at the Basilica of St. Peter's and the canopy over the altar at St. Paul Outside the Walls.
Cassius Dio	(ca. 155–235) sometimes known as Dio Cassius, wrote an 80-volume history of Rome beginning with its legendary founding up to the then present day.
Charlemagne	(ca. 742–814), emperor of the Holy Roman Empire, crowned emperor in the basilica of St. Peter on Christmas eve in 800 by Pope St. Leo III.
Cicero	(106 BCE–43 BCE) Prolific Roman philosopher, statesman, politician, and lawyer influential in late days of the Republic. Considered one of the greatest orators in Roman history.
Constantine	(285–337) proclaimed emperor in York in 306 upon his father's death (Constantius I). Constantine then went about consolidating power and eliminating enemies, including defeating Maxentius at the Milvian Bridge in 312. Issued the

APPENDICES

	Edict of Milan, a policy of religious tolerance for Christianity, in 313. Finally became sole emperor in 324 and moved the capital to Byzantium which he renamed Constantinople. He called the council of Nicea in 325 and was eventually baptized a Christian on his deathbed.
Eusebius	(ca. 260–340) considered the father of church history, author of *Ecclesiastical History*, *Life of Constantine*, and other works.
Gallio	(5 BCE–65 CE) Roman senator and elder brother of Seneca. Gallio was proconsul of Achaia when the Apostle Paul was haled before him. Likely committed suicide shortly after Seneca's doing the same.
Germanicus	(15 BCE–19 CE) Roman general who conquered German tribes in the time of Tiberius, and was adopted by the same in 4 CE. He married Agrippina the elder, and together they had nine children among whom was Gaius (Caligula) and Agrippina the younger. Germanicus was also the brother of Claudius, and grandfather of Nero.
Herod Agrippa	(10 BCE–44 CE) grandson of Herod the Great. Ties to the Roman imperial family (Caligula and Claudius), named after Marcus Agrippa. Persecuted the church in Jerusalem (Acts 12:1–23).
Herod Agrippa II	(27–93 CE) son of Herod Agrippa. Agrippa II and his sister Berenice heard Paul's case at Caesarea Maritima. Agrippa II supported Vespasian during the Jerusalem Revolt and lived many of his remaining years in Rome with Berenice, after receiving awards from the emperor for loyalty.
Herod Antipas	(20 BCE–39 CE) son of Herod the Great, named to the throne upon his father's death by Augustus in 1 BCE. Uncle to Herod Agrippa. Antipas divorced

his first wife in favor of Herodias who had been married to his half-brother Herod II. John the Baptist condemned this action of Herod Antipas, and was subsequently arrested and beheaded. According to the Gospel of Luke, Antipas also played a role in the trial of Jesus. Antipas was exiled to Gaul after being accused by his nephew Herod Agrippa of a conspiracy against Caligula.

Herod the Great — (73 BCE–4 BCE) King of Judea installed by Rome. Expanded the Temple, constructed Caesarea Maritima, Masada, and Herodium. The Herod of the "Massacre of the Innocents" in Matthew's Gospel.

Horace — (65 BCE–8 BCE) Poet and satirist during the reign of Augustus.

Ignatius of Antioch — (?–ca. 108 CE) an "Apostolic Father" and bishop of Antioch in Syria who was taken in chains to Rome to face martyrdom, writing letters to various churches and to Polycarp along the way.

Ignatius of Loyola — (1491–1556) founder of the Jesuits (Society of Jesus). Motto is "ad maiorem dei gloriam," for the greater glory of God, abbreviated as AMDG.

Irenaeus — (ca 120–202) bishop of Lyons, who heard Polycarp as a youth. Wrote influential works giving an insight into early Christianity.

Jerome — (347–420) baptized in Rome about 360, Jerome eventually settled in Bethlehem in 386, where he led a life of austerity and study. He was a prolific writer and translated the Scriptures into Latin, which we call the Vulgate.

John Chrysostom — (349–407) Great Christian preacher and Archbishop of Constantinople, known as the "golden-tongued," yet composed a series of homilies, "Against the Jews."

APPENDICES

John, son of Levi, of Giscala (?–post 70 CE)
: Leader of the zealots during the Jewish revolution against Rome. Taken prisoner and brought to Rome to be displayed in the triumph.

Josephus, Flavius
: (37–100 CE) Galilean Jew who led Jewish forces against Rome until he was captured, when he prophesied Vespasian would become emperor of the world. He then assisted the Romans with the siege and destruction of Jerusalem before settling in Rome and writing histories as a patron of the Flavian emperors.

Maderno, Carlo
: (1556–1629) architect responsible for the nave and façade of St. Peter's, including the stuccoes in the portico, among other works in Rome.

Maxentius
: (?–312) son of emperor Maximian (r. 286–305), proclaimed western emperor in 306 at Rome. He was defeated by Constantine at the Battle of the Milvian Bridge on Oct 28, 312 where he was also drowned.

Michelangelo
: (1475–1564) Perhaps most famous sculptor, architect, painter and artist of the Renaissance. His major works in Rome include: Dome of St. Peter, Church of Sta. Maria degli Angeli, Pietà, the Last Judgment and the ceiling in the Sistine Chapel, Moses at San Pietro in Vincoli, Risen Christ at Santa Maria Sopra Minerva, and the steps at the Campidoglio.

Luther, Martin
: (1483–1546) Catholic priest who became the premier force behind the "Protestant Reformation" with his 95 theses, fueled in part by the Renovation of St. Peter's and the fundraising efforts for that project.

Octavian
: (63 BCE–14 CE) great nephew, adopted son and heir of Julius Caesar. Founder of Imperial Rome.

	Proclaimed "Augustus" by the Roman Senate in 27 BCE after he defeated Mark Antony and Cleopatra and consolidated power to himself.
Origen	(ca. 185–254 CE) Origen led a long and distinguished career in writing and commenting on the Scriptures. He traveled extensively, teaching and preaching in many different cities. Perhaps the most learned Christian from the time of Paul to the time of Augustine.
Papias	(ca. 70–163 CE) Considered an "Apostolic Father." Bishop of Hierapolis (in modern day Turkey). He wrote "The Sayings of the Lord," which is quoted by Irenaeus, Eusebius and others. Papias is said to have been a "hearer of John and a companion of Polycarp" (AH 5.33.4).
Pliny (the elder)	(23–79 CE) Roman author, administrator, and naval commander who wrote the thirty-seven book, ten volume work, *Natural History* which was dedicated to Vespasian his close friend and then Emperor. Pliny died in the eruption of Vesuvius when he went to explore a 'unusual cloud' 'like an umbrella pine' emanating from the mountain, according to his nephew Pliny the younger.
Polycarp	(69–155 CE) Bishop of Smyrna. Disciple of John. Author of a Letter to the Philippians. Subject of the "Martyrdom of Polycarp." As a youth, Irenaeus heard Polycarp speak.
Presbyter (the)	(ca. late first century, early second century CE) The Presbyter John is mentioned by Papias as quoted by Eusebius. The Presbyter John is often named with Aristion, as two disciples (not apostles) of the Lord.
Raphael	(1483–1520) Painter and architect whose short life belied his prodigious work. Perhaps more known in Rome for his paintings, especially at the Vatican, he was a principal architect of St. Peter's though his

plans were essentially discarded by his successor on the project, Michelangelo. Raphael's tomb is in the Pantheon.

Seneca (the younger) — (4 BCE–65 CE) philosopher, tutor and advisor to Nero eventually compelled to commit suicide by the same Emperor. Seneca's older brother was Gallio, proconsul of Achaia. Their father was Seneca the elder.

Simon bar Giora — (Simon, son of Gioras; CE ?–post 70) Leader of the sicarii faction during Jewish revolt against Rome. Captured and brought to Rome; said to have been imprisoned at the Mamertine before being publicly executed at the Capitoline.

Simon Magus — Baptized by Philip the deacon, Simon Magus is a character in Acts of the Apostles who interacted with Peter (Acts 8:9–24) and attempted to purchase the power of the Holy Spirit (from which we have the term, "simony" i.e., the attempt to purchase position or influence in the church). From that episode Simon Magus became an antagonist of Peter in apocryphal literature, especially the Acts of Peter. Some church fathers consider Simon Magus to have been the source of every heresy.

Tacitus — (ca. 55–ca. 120 CE) Roman historian, senator, and friend of Pliny the younger. His Annals tell the story of the early Empire, including the great fire of Rome in the time of Nero.

Bibliography

The headings Ancient, Medieval, Reformation, and Modern in the bibliography refer to the general time period of the source material rather than the date of the book that contains the source material. For example, though Martial's *Spectacles* are from a 1993 edition, he wrote in the first century. Therefore, his work appears under the heading, "Ancient."

Ancient

Bibliographical data is given for translations used in this book. Various editions are available for most of these works.

Appian. *Civil Wars*. In *Appian, Roman History, Volume III: The Civil Wars, Books 1–3.26*. Translated by Horace White. LCL 4. Cambridge, MA: Harvard University Press, 1913.

Cassius Dio. *Roman History*. In *Roman History, Volume VIII: Books 61-70*. Translated by Earnest Cary and Herbert B. Foster. LCL 176. Cambridge, MA: Harvard University Press, 1925.

Cicero. *Pro Quinctio. Pro Roscio Amerino. Pro Roscio Comoedo. On the Agrarian Law*. Translated by J. H. Freese. LCL 240. Cambridge, MA: Harvard University Press, 1930.

Clement. "First Letter of Clement to the Corinthians." In *The Apostolic Fathers, Volume I: I Clement. II Clement. Ignatius. Polycarp. Didache*. Edited and translated by Bart D. Ehrman. LCL 24. Cambridge, MA: Harvard University Press, 2003.

Eusebius. *Ecclesiastical History*. In *Ecclesiastical History, Volume I: Books 1–5*. Translated by Kirsopp Lake. LCL 153. Cambridge, MA: Harvard University Press, 1926.

———. *Life of Constantine*. Translated by Averil Cameron and Stuart G. Hall. Clarendon Ancient History. Oxford: Oxford University Press, 1999.

Ignatius of Antioch. *Letter to the Romans*. In *The Apostolic Fathers, Volume I: I Clement. II Clement. Ignatius. Polycarp. Didache*. Edited and translated by Bart D. Ehrman. LCL 24. Cambridge, MA: Harvard University Press, 2003.

Irenaeus. *Against the Heresies*. Translated by Dominic J. Unger. ACW 65. Mahwah, NJ: Paulist, 1992.

BIBLIOGRAPHY

Josephus. *Jewish Antiquities.* In *Jewish Antiquities, Volume VIII: Books 18-19.* Translated by Louis H. Feldman. LCL 433. Cambridge, MA: Harvard University Press, 1965.

———. *Jewish Antiquities.* In *Jewish Antiquities, Volume IX: Book 20.* Translated by Louis H. Feldman. LCL 456. Cambridge, MA: Harvard University Press, 1965.

———. *The Jewish War.* In *The Jewish War, Volume III: Books 5-7.* Translated by H. St. J. Thackeray. LCL 210. Cambridge, MA: Harvard University Press, 1928.

———. *The Jewish War.* In *Josephus: The Jewish War*, edited by G. A. Williamson. Rev. ed. New York: Penguin, 1970.

Justin Martyr. *Dialogue with Trypho.* Edited by Alexander Roberts, James Donaldson, and A. Cleveland Coxe. Translated by Marcus Dods and George Reith. Ante-Nicene Fathers 1. Buffalo, NY: Christian Literature, 1885.

Macrobius. *Saturnalia.* In *Saturnalia, Volume I: Books 1-2.* Edited and translated by Robert A. Kaster. LCL 510. Cambridge, MA: Harvard University Press, 2011.

Martial. *Epigrams, Volume I: Spectacles, Books 1-5.* Edited and translated by D. R. Shackleton Bailey. LCL 94. Cambridge, MA: Harvard University Press, 1993.

———. *Epigrams, Volume II: Books 6-10.* Edited and translated by D. R. Shackleton Bailey. LCL 95. Cambridge, MA: Harvard University Press, 1993.

———. *Epigrams, Volume III: Books 11-14.* Edited and translated by D. R. Shackleton Bailey. LCL 480. Cambridge, MA: Harvard University Press, 1993.

Origen. *Contra Celsum.* Edited and translated by Henry Chadwick. Cambridge: Cambridge University Press, 1980.

Philo. *De opificio mundi.* In *On the Creation. Allegorical Interpretation of Genesis 2 and 3.* Translated by F. H. Colson, G. H. Whitaker. LCL 226. Cambridge, MA: Harvard University Press, 1929.

Pliny. *Natural History.* In *Natural History, Volume X: Books 36-37.* Translated by D. E. Eichholz. LCL 419. Cambridge, MA: Harvard University Press, 1962.

Quintilian. *Institutes of Oratory.* In Quintilian. *The Orator's Education*, Volume II: Books 3-5. Edited and translated by Donald A. Russell. LCL 125. Cambridge, MA: Harvard University Press, 2002.

Sallust. *The War with Catiline.* In *The War with Catiline. The War with Jugurtha.* Edited by John T. Ramsey. Translated by J. C. Rolfe. LCL 116. Cambridge, MA: Harvard University Press, 2013.

Seneca. *Epistles.* In *Epistles, Volume I: Epistles 1-65.* Translated by Richard M. Gummere. LCL 75. Cambridge, MA: Harvard University Press, 1917.

Suetonius. *Lives of the Caesars.* In *Lives of the Caesars, Volume II: Claudius. Nero. Galba, Otho, and Vitellius. Vespasian. Titus, Domitian. Lives of Illustrious Men: Grammarians and Rhetoricians. Poets (Terence. Virgil. Horace. Tibullus. Persius. Lucan). Lives of Pliny the Elder and Passienus Crispus.* Translated by J. C. Rolfe. LCL 38. Cambridge, MA: Harvard University Press, 1914.

Tacitus. *The Annals of Imperial Rome.* In *Annals: Books 13-16.* Translated by John Jackson. LCL 322. Cambridge, MA: Harvard University Press, 1937.

Tertullian. *Apology.* In *Tertullian, Minucius Felix:* Apology. De Spectaculis. *Minucius Felix:* Octavius. Translated by T. R. Glover and Gerald H. Rendall. LCL 250. Cambridge, MA: Harvard University Press, 1931.

———. *On Baptism.* Edited by Alexander Roberts, James Donaldson, and A. Cleveland Coxe. Translated by S. Thelwall. ANF 3. Buffalo, NY: Christian Literature, 1885.

———. *On Modesty.* Edited by Alexander Roberts, James Donaldson, and A. Cleveland Coxe. Translated by S. Thelwall. ANF 4. Buffalo, NY: Christian Literature, 1885.

———. *Prescription of the Heretics.* Edited by Alexander Roberts, James Donaldson, and A. Cleveland Coxe. Translated by S. Thelwall. *ANF* 3. Buffalo, NY: Christian Literature, 1885.

———. *Scorpiace.* Edited by Alexander Roberts, James Donaldson, and A. Cleveland Coxe. Translated by S. Thelwall. *ANF* 3. Buffalo, NY: Christian Literature, 1885.

Varro. *On the Latin Language, Volume I: Books 5–7.* Translated by Roland G. Kent. LCL 333. Cambridge, MA: Harvard University Press, 1938.

Medieval (Early to Late)

Augustine. *City of God, Volume VI: Books 18.36–20.* Translated by William Chase Greene. LCL 416. Cambridge, MA: Harvard University Press, 1960.

———. *Confessions, Volume I: Books 1–8.* Translated by Carolyn J.-B. Hammond. LCL 26. Cambridge, MA: Harvard University Press, 2014.

———. *On Christian Doctrine.* Translated by J. F. Shaw. Mineola, NY: Dover, 2009.

Davis, Raymond, *The Book of Pontiffs (Liber Pontificalis): The Ancient Biographies of The First Ninety Roman Bishops to AD 715.* TTHLS 5. Liverpool: Liverpool University Press, 1989.

De Voragine, Jacobus, and William Granger Ryan. *The Golden Legend Readings on the Saints.* Princeton: Princeton University Press, 2012.

Duchesne, L., and Cyrille Vogel. *Le Liber Pontificalis.* Bibliothèque Des Écoles Françaises d'Athènes et de Rome. Paris: E. Thorin, 1957.

Fischer, Bonifatius, and Robert Weber, eds. *Biblia Sacra: Iuxta Vulgatam Versionem.* Quartam Emendatam edition. Stuttgart: Deutsche Bibelgesellschaft, 1994.

Gardiner, E. *The Marvels of Rome. Mirabilia Urbis Romae.* 2nd ed. New York: Italica, 1986.

Gregory I. *Gregory the Great: Forty Gospel Homilies.* Translated by D. Hurst. CSS 123. Kalamazoo, MI: Cistercian, 1990.

Jerome. *St. Jerome: Commentary on Ezekiel.* Edited and translated by Thomas P. Scheck. ACW 71. Mahwah, NJ: Newman, 2017.

Lipsius, Richard Adelbert, Max Bonnet, and Heinz Kraft. *Acta Apostolorum Apocrypha Post Constantinum Tischendorf.* Hildesheim: Hildesheim, G. Olms, 1972.

Martyn, John R. C. *The Letters of Gregory the Great.* MST 40. Toronto: Pontifical Institute of Mediaeval Studies, 2004.

Nichols, Francis Morgan, trans. *Mirabilia Urbis Romae: The Marvels of Rome or A Picture of the Golden City. An English Version of the Medieval Guide-Book with a Supplement of Illustrative Matter and Notes.* London: Ellis and Elvey/Spithoever, 1889.

Reformation/Renaissance

Fontana, Carlo, et al. *Templum Vaticanum Et Ipsius Origo.* 1694.

Luther, Martin, "On the Jews and Their Lies." In *Luther's Works* 47. Edited by Helmut T. Lehmann and Franklin Sherman. Translated by Martin H. Bertram. Philadelphia: Fortress, 1971.

———. *Works of Martin Luther.* Edited and translated by Adolph Spaeth, L. D. Reed, Henry Eyster Jacobs, et al. Philadelphia: A. J. Holman, 1915.

Mombrizio, Bonino. *Sanctuarium seu Vitae Sanctorum.* Vol. 2. Fontemoing: Paris, 1910.

BIBLIOGRAPHY

Modern

Aicher, Peter J. *Rome Alive*. 2 vols. Wauconda, IL: Bolchazy-Carducci, 2004.
Barnes, Arthur Stapylton. *The Martyrdom of St. Peter and St. Paul*. New York: Oxford University Press, 1933.
———. *St. Peter in Rome and His Tomb on the Vatican Hill*. London: Swan Sonnenschein, 1900.
Berenson, Bernard. *The Arch of Constantine or the Decline of Form*. New York: MacMillan, 1954.
Boyle, Leonard. *A Short Guide to St. Clement's*. Rome: Collegio San Clemente, 1989.
Boyle, Leonard E., et al. *San Clemente Miscellany II: Art and Archaeology*. Rome: Apud S. Clementem, 1978.
Brown, Raymond, and John P. Meier. *Antioch and Rome: New Testament Cradles of Catholic Christianity*. New York, NY: Paulist Press, 1983.
Casson, Lionel. *Everyday Life in Ancient Rome*. Rev. and expanded ed. Baltimore: Johns Hopkins University Press, 1998.
Cook, John Granger. *Roman Attitudes Toward the Christians: From Claudius to Hadrian*. Tübingen: Mohr Siebeck, 2010.
Cullman, Oscar. *Peter: Disciple—Apostle—Martyr*. Translated by F. V. Filson. Philadelphia: Westminster, 1953.
Della Portella, Ivana. *Subterranean Rome*. Venice: Arsenale, 1999.
Eastman, David L. *The Ancient Martyrdom Accounts of Peter and Paul*. Edited by Craig A Gibson et al. WGRW 39. Atlanta: Society of Biblical Literature, 2015.
———. *Paul the Martyr: The Cult of the Apostle in the Latin West*. Edited by John T. Fitzgerald. WGRWSS 4. Atlanta: Society of Biblical Literature, 2011.
Ehrman, Bart. *Peter, Paul, and Mary Magdalene: The Followers of Jesus in History and Legend*. Oxford: Oxford University Press, 2008.
Elliott, John H. *1 Peter*. AYBC 37B. New Haven, CT: Yale University Press, 2000.
Fehl, Philipp. "Michaelangelo's Crucifixion of St. Peter: Notes on the Identification of the Locale of the Action." *The Art Bulletin* 53/3 (September 1971) 326–43.
Finch, Margaret. "Petrine Landmarks in Two Predella Panels by Jacopo di Cione." *Artibus et Historiae* 12/23 (1991) 67–82.
Fitzmyer, Joseph A. *Romans: A New Translation with Introduction and Commentary*. AYBC 32. New Haven, CT: Yale University Press, 2007.
Gibbon, Edward. *The Autobiography of Edward Gibbon*. London: Oxford University Press, 1907.
Gowers, E. "Horace, *Satires* 1.5: An Inconsequential Journey." *PCPS* 39 (1993) 48–66.
Guidobaldi, Federico, and Paul Lawlor. *La Basilica e l'area archeologica di s. Clemente in Roma*. Rome: Apud s. Clementum, 1990.
Hopkins, Keith, and Mary Beard. *The Colosseum*. Wonders of the World. Cambridge, MA: Harvard University Press, 2005.
Huskinson, J. M. "The Crucifixion of St. Peter: A Fifteenth-Century Topographical Problem." *Journal of the Warburg and Courtauld Institutes* 32 (1969) 135–61.
———. Review of *Est et alia pyramis*, by M. Demus-Quatember. *The Art Bulletin* 58/4 (1976) 618–21.
Johnson, Luke Timothy. *The First and Second Letters to Timothy: A New Translation with Introduction and Commentary*. AYBC 35A. New Haven, CT: Yale University Press, 2001.

BIBLIOGRAPHY

Jones, Brian W. *The Emperor Domitian*. London: Routledge, 1992.

Jones, Peter, and Keith Sidwell, eds. *The World of Rome: An Introduction to Roman Culture*. New York: Cambridge University Press, 1997.

Kelly, J. N. D. *The Oxford Dictionary of Popes*. Oxford: Oxford University Press, 1986.

Kiel, Micah. "Did Paul Get Whacked? The Endings of *The Sopranos* and the Acts of the Apostles." *SBL Forum*. June 2007. http://sbl-site.org/Article.aspx?ArticleID=695

Lampe, Peter. *From Paul to Valentinus: Christians at Rome in the First Two Centuries*. Minneapolis: Augsburg Fortress, 2003.

Lanciani, Rodolfo, *Pagan and Christian Rome*. Cambridge, MA: Houghton, Mifflin, 1893.

Lloyd, Joan E. Barclay. *Ss. Vincenzo e Anastasio at Tre Fontane: History and Architecture of a Medieval Cistercian Abbey*. CSS 188. Kalamazoo, MI: Cistercian, 2006.

Lowrie, Walter. *Ss. Peter and Paul in Rome: An Archaeological Rhapsody*. New York: Oxford University Press, 1940.

Macadam, Alta, and A. B. Barber. *Rome*. 11th ed. Somerset: Blue Guides, 2016.

MacDonald, William L. *The Pantheon*. Cambridge, MA: Harvard University Press, 1976.

Masson, Georgina. *The Companion Guide to Rome*. Revised by John Fort. 8th ed. Rochester, NY: Companion, 2003.

McBrien, Richard. *Lives of the Popes: The Pontiffs from St. Peter to John Paul II*. San Francisco: Harper Collins, 1997.

Merton, Thomas. *The Seven Storey Mountain*. Orlando: Mariner, 1998.

Miller, Keith. *Saint Peter's*. Wonders of the World. Cambridge, MA: Harvard University Press, 2007.

Morgan, Gwyn. *69 A.D.: The Year of the Four Emperors*. New York: Oxford University Press, 2007.

Morton, H. V. *In the Steps of St. Paul*. Cambridge, MA: Da Capo, 2002.

———. *A Traveller in Rome*. Cambridge, MA: Da Capo, 2002.

O'Connor, Daniel William. *Peter in Rome: The Literary, Liturgical, and Archeological Evidence*. New York: Columbia University Press, 1969.

Papi, Donatella. *San Pietro in Vaticano*. Rome: Elio De Rosa, 2001.

Petersen, Joan M. "The Identification of the Titulus Fasciolae and Its Connection with Pope Gregory the Great." *Vigiliae Christianae* 30/2 (June 1976) 151–58.

Platner, Samuel Ball. *The Topography and Monuments of Ancient Rome*. 2nd ed. Boston: Allyn & Bacon, 1911.

San Pietro in Vaticano. *Roma Sacra: Guide to the Churches in the Eternal City*. Itineraries 21–22. Elio de Rosa, 1995.

Schneemelcher, W. *New Testament Apocrypha*. 2 vols. Translated by R. McLachlan Wilson. Louisville: Westminster/John Knox, 1991.

Scotti, Rita A. *Basilica: The Splendor and the Scandal: Building St. Peter's*. New York: Penguin, 2006.

Snyder, Graydon F. *Ante Pacem: Archeological Evidence of Church Life Before Constantine*. Macon, GA: Mercer University Press, 2003.

Southern, Pat. *Domitian: Tragic Tyrant*. Bloomington: Indiana University Press, 1997.

Sweet, Waldo E., *Lectiones Secundae*. Artes Latinae. Level Two. Wauconda, IL: Bolchazy-Carducci, 1996.

Tajra, H. W. *The Martyrdom of St. Paul: Historical and Judicial Context, Traditions, and Legends*. WUNT: Reihe 2.67. Tubingen: Mohr Siebeck, 1994.

Toynbee, Joyce, and John Ward Perkins. *The Shrine of Saint Peter and the Vatican Excavations*. New York: Pantheon, 1957.

BIBLIOGRAPHY

Tylenda, Joseph N. *The Pilgrim's Guide to Rome's Principal Churches*. Collegeville, MN: Liturgical, 1993.

Ulansey, David. *The Origin of the Mithraic Mysteries*. Oxford: Oxford University Press, 1991.

Valentini, Roberto, and Giuseppe Zucchetti. *Codice topografico della città di Roma*. Vol. 4. Rome: Tipografia del Senato, 1953.

www.ingramcontent.com/pod-product-compliance
Lightning Source LLC
Chambersburg PA
CBHW051744230426
43670CB00012B/2156